Experience of a Confederate Chaplain

1861-1865

By Rev. A. D. Betts, D. D.
N. C. Conference
Methodist Episcopal Church, South

Chaplain
30th N. C. Troops

Edited by W. A. Betts

REPRINTED BY
The Scuppernong Press
Wake Forest, NC
www.scuppernongpress.com

Experience of a Confederate Chaplain 1861-1865
By Rev. A. D. Betts, D. D.

Edited by W. A. Betts and Frank B. Powell, III

©2023 The Scuppernong Press

First Printing

The Scuppernong Press
PO Box 1724
Wake Forest, NC 27588
www.scuppernongpress.com

Cover and Book design by Frank B. Powell, III

All rights reserved

Printed in the United States of America

No part of this book may be reproduced or transmitted in any form or by any means, electronic or mechanical, including photocopying, recording, or by any information and storage and retrieval system, without written permission from the editor and/or publisher.

International Standard Book Number ISBN 978-1-942806-50-9

Library of Congress Control Number: 2023932224

CONTENTS

Foreword v
Confederate Chaplains vii
Rev. A. D. Betts ix
Introduction xi
The War of the Confederacy xiii
Experience of A Confederate Chaplain 1
First Letters of Condolence 3
Getting a Furlough 13
Getting Home! Five Days! 13
Getting to Conference 14
1863. Thank God! 14
Boxes for the Soldiers 49
My First Interview with a Federal Soldier on Duty 53
Apologia 55
Biographical 63
Eighth Annual Meeting and Reunion
   of the United Confederate Veterans 64
The Ninth of April 1865 66
The Bivouac of the Dead 67
All Quiet Along the Potomac 68
To the Confederate Dead 69
Little Giffen 70
The Conquered Banner 72
Dixie 73
Land of the South 74
The Old North State 76
Ho! For Carolina 77
Apple of Gold in Pictures of Silver 78
Rev. W. A. Betts 81

FOREWORD

Experience of A Confederate Chaplain is a great book which gives us a first-hand look at what chaplains had to do to serve the spiritual needs of troops in the field. Little is heard or written about chaplains during the War for Southern Independence. We all know they existed, but we have no idea the hardships, dedication and devotion of Confederate Chaplains. In fact, the military didn't even support chaplains in the beginning, so they had to fund their own service and supplies.

This small book is quite a treasure for modern day readers and researchers, especially in these days of revisionist history. Here is a first hand account from someone who was there and lived during the War in the field. He saw it and wrote about it.

I really admire Reverend Betts' devotion and dedication, qualities sorely lacking in the twenty-first century. He saw so many men die, many of them friends, during his time in service. I don't know how he was able to carry on. He left his family to serve and you can tell by his writings, he missed them greatly.

As you read Betts' day-to-day entries, I'm sure you will gain admiration for his service as I did.

The book ends with some songs and poetry which were popular during the War, but rarely seen today.

This edition is reprinted in a modern typeface with small changes to modern punctuation and grammar standards. Most of the illustrations are included as printed in the original edition.

We hope you enjoy reading Reverend Bett's story as much as we did.

— Frank B. Powell, III
Editor

Rev. A .D. Betts, Chaplain, 30th Regiment.
Rev. L. A. Bikle, Chaplain, 20th Regiment.
Rev. A. A. Watson, Chaplain, 2nd Regiment.
Rev. A. W. Mangum, Chaplain, 6th Regiment.
5 Rev. A. L. Stough, Chaplain, 37th Regiment.
6 Rev. William S. Lacy, Chaplain, 47th Regiment.
7 Rev. R. S. Webb, Chaplain, 44th Regiment.

Experience of a Confederate Chaplain 1861–1865

Rev. A. D. BETTS, D. D.

of the

North Carolina Conference, Methodist Episcopal Church, South

Experience of a Confederate Chaplain 1861–1865

INTRODUCTION

HISTORY rightly defined is more than a narration of events transpiring within certain periods of the Calendar. That most useful of the sciences deals with the philosophy and results of occurrences, deriving there from an array of principles which form a part of the world's necessary and priceless treasure. The historian takes the crude materials time pours into his hands, digests, filters and refines the mass, thereby securing the simplest and most serviceable products. These he places on the market where buyers always wait, eager and affluent. Artists and artisans these buyers are, who for their own and others' wellbeing build structures, weave fabrics, or portray the perfect pattern.

The chronicles of a Confederate Chaplain's diary will doubtless furnish the staple for weaving a most engaging story when the true historian shall find them.

The perusal of these plain annals will surely revive in the memory of many a Confederate Veteran the vivid panorama of that unequaled and heroic struggle for the perpetuation of certain principles that underlie the purest and best form of government in the estimation of loyal Southrons.

It is devoutly desired that all who may trace the indentures of this diary will reflect gratefully upon the all wise and gracious providence of God which seeks to save even unto the uttermost. It is believed many persons, at home and in the army, were led to accept Christ as their Saviour, who under other circumstances might never have known His forgiving love.

Joseph T. Derry in his *"Story of the Confederate States,"* says:

"There was throughout the Southern army a strong religious sentiment, and many of the officers and men were deeply pious. ***** Firmly believing that God gave to them all the brilliant victories that shed such lustre on their arms, they also believed that God in His wisdom had given them final defeat. It is this feeling that has caused the Southern people, without any consciousness of guilt, or shame, to accept in perfect good faith the result of the war and the changed order of things, and at the same time to use every constitutional method to maintain the rights of their States as co-equal members of the Union."

W. A. B.

THE WAR OF THE CONFEDERACY

EDITORIAL NOTE

The discriminating minds among our intelligent young people of the South will readily perceive that there is a manifest and important, because truthful, distinction to be maintained touching the style and title of the conflict waged on this American continent during 1861-1865, between The United States and the newly born nationality known as The Confederate States. The following from Dr. S. A. Steel, of Richmond, Va., will be appreciated:

"The term 'Civil War' ought to be abandoned because it embodies an error. A civil war is a war between factions contending for the control of the same government, like Caesar and Pompey, like Lancaster and York. If the Southern people had fought in the Union, it would have been a civil war, and the defeated party would have been rebels. The movement was a revolution. The object of it was to maintain a separate government. The war was between the government of the United States and the government of the Confederate States. We went out of the Union; went so completely that we had to be re-admitted. We were not 'rebels,' but patriots, wisely or unwisely, exercising the inalienable right of self-government in an honest effort to rectify political difficulties. This is the verdict history will ultimately pronounce upon that struggle."

While our friends, the enemy, persist in calling us "Rebels," and refer to that struggle for Southern independence as "The Rebellion," we are content to bear the obloquy, knowing the injustice of it; yea, we glory in it, as did the now largest of protestant religious denominations accept and wear the term of reproach designating them "Methodists." But let us not forget that "We be brethren!"

Greenville, South Carolina.

EXPERIENCE OF A CONFEDERATE CHAPLAIN
1861-1865

One day in April, 1861, I heard President Lincoln had called on the State troops to force the seceding States back into the Union. That was one of the saddest days of my life. I had prayed and hoped that war might be averted. I had loved the Union, and clung to it. That day I saw war was inevitable. The inevitable must be met. That day I walked up and down my porch in Smithville (now Southport, N. C.) and wept and suffered and prayed for the South.

The drum and fife were soon heard there, and all through the Old North State companies of our best men, young and middle aged, offered themselves to the Governor of the State. He organized them into regiments. The 20th Regiment was soon sent to Smithville. Rev. T. M. Sprunt, D. D., was their Chaplain. (See history in "Chaplain Service.") Brunswick County had a company (G) in this regiment. As I had preached in that county in 1859, I knew some of the men. The parents of Capt. John S. Brooks were very dear friends to me. The Captain went safely through all the perils till 1864, when he was killed, having been promoted to Major.

John Harvil was killed in 1862.

Brunswick soon had another company ready for service. That was put in the 30th Regiment with "A" from Sampson, "B" from Warren, "D" from Wake, "E" from Duplin, "F" from Pitt, "G" from Granville, "H" from Moore, "I" from Nash, and "K" from Mecklenburg County. As I had preached in Sampson County in 1857 and 1858 1 found friends in Company A. Among my friends in Company C was Lorenzo Dow Cain from Bladen. He had been teaching some time in Brunswick before the war, and joined Capt. Joseph Green's company and was commissioned 2nd Lieut., on the day that most of the men enlisted — Sept. 26th, 1861. He was a bright, amiable young man.

When the 30th Regiment was organized at Raleigh some one proposed that the commissioned officers should call a chaplain. Lieut. Cain wrote me from Raleigh that they had chosen Me, and urged me to accept, modestly suggesting that it would give me a field for large usefulness. I prayed over it a few days and wrote to Governor Clark that I would accept. My commission was dated October 25th, 1861. The 30th Regiment was soon sent to Smithville. I reported for duty. Col. F. M. Parker kindly allowed me to finish up my work on the circuit and go to Conference at Louisburg.

There three others had an experience with me. A noble citizen put us in a nice new house. One night we left our house unlocked while we were out. Rev. R. A. Willis lost his trunk, with books, clothes and manuscript sermons. Rev. J. H. Robbins lost his overcoat. Rev. R. S. Webb lost his valise and clothes. My carpet bag and clothing were gone too. We hired a detective to hunt our lost goods. One day we heard a valise had been seen on some drift wood in Tar River. We hastened to the spot. As we crossed a field we saw sheets of paper among the briars. They were Brother Willis' sermons. We walked on picking the sheets from the briars. Bro. Webb, in a solemn, dry tone, said: Bro. Willis sows "beside all waters." Bro. Willis did not laugh. We found a shirt for me and a garment or two for others.

My regiment was moved to Camp Wyatt, on Federal Point. I rented a house near by for wife and three children. I preached often and held prayer meeting in some company almost every night. I copied rolls of companies, noting age of each soldier, where born, post office, creed, and to what local church each belonged, married or single, number of children if any, etc.

In the spring of 1862 the regiment was ordered to White Oak River, Onslow County.

J. W. Russ, of Bladen, asked me to send my family to board with him. I sent them.

Regiment was reorganized in May and ordered to Richmond in June, reaching there June 15th.

June 23rd I saw the first wounded of my regiment, A. A. Lewis, of Sampson County, and Dr. Grissom, of Wake County.

June 25th we heard frequent cannonading— 30 per minute.

Thursday, June 26th, I was sick in my tent. Before day I heard such noise as I had never heard before. Everything in motion, troops, troops, wagons, wagons, artillery, artillery. Heard cannons from 5 p. m. to 6 p. m.., 30 per minute; at 7:30, 40 per minute. Too unwell to go to my men. Heard constant musketry. Oh, that I could be there to comfort the wounded and dying, and to encourage the fighting.

Friday, June 27th, Dr. Campbell and I start at 4 a. m. to try to join our regiment.

At Mechanicsville we saw many wounded, and at Mills, many dead and wounded. Among the dead I saw the handsome form of my noble school-mate, James A. Wright, of Wilmington.

Unable to reach our brigade we drop back through Ewell's and Stonewall Jackson's commands, and carry Captain Drake toward our old camp. Sleep under a tree. Our Regiment lost some men — S. Tedder, A. B. Hood and A. F. Steel of Mecklenburg.

Sunday, June 29th — Pray in camp, and pray with them, and carry Capt. Drake to Richmond.

FIRST LETTERS OF CONDOLENCE

Write to Mrs. Tedder and Mrs. Hood, whose husbands had fallen.

July 3rd — In camp sick. Meet Revs. T. J. Gattis and J. C. Brent of North Carolina. Learn that Bro. E. J. Grear of Company "C," was badly wounded and captured. He had left his pocket book containing $42.21 with me. I wish he had it in gold.

July 4th — Once a National Jubilee? With Brother Gattis visit Captains Brooks and Stanley. Visit Chimborazo Hospital, some of 30th Regiment, Lieut. Angus Shaw of 38th Regiment, D. Danford of Company "C," and others at Seabrook Hospital. See Jos. Mason's left leg cut off below the knee. Brother Gattis spends night with me in camp.

July 6th — Letter from wife; she may come next Tuesday! Walk, walk, walk, visit wounded soldiers, Camp Winder and other Hospitals, Thos. Whitted and Captain Svkes of Bladen, many friends and many poor strangers. Some will live, others will die. Reach camp late, very tired. Cough and cold very bad.

July 7th — Visit Swift Galloway of Brunswick, Daniel McDugald of Cumberland, J. Mason, etc., etc. A telegram from Wilmington says Mrs. Betts is on her way. God bring her safely!

July 8th — Wife and three children arrive. Sister Galloway comes on to see Swift. About 8 p. m. my son Willie (under 5 years) falls from his grandpa's porch six or seven feet and cuts his head fearfully on a brick.

July 9th — Willie is doing well. McDugald about to die. Lieut. Shaw very low. Swift Galloway doing well. Visit D. H. Neal. Piper, and Horace Morrison.

July 11th — Rain all the morning. Walkout through mud to camp, and find regiment returned after seven days in fighting and suffering. Glad to see Col. Parker once more. Return weary to Pa's, having walked nine and rode three miles.

Sunday, July 13th — In ramp. Overtax my strength.

July 14th — Feeble. Visit a few wounded.

July 15th — Ride to camp and visit my sick. Daniel McDugald, my school-mate three years at Summerville and my class-mate three years at Chapel Hill, has died of wounds.

July 16th— Keep close. Suffer with cough. Married Thos. E. Amos and Sarah G. Davis, in Clay St. Church, Richmond.

July 17th — Find Lieut. Grier at Dunlop and Moncure Hospital, badly wounded. Glad to see the good man. Ride to camp and spend night on ground.

July 18th— Ride to Pa's. Wife and I visit Lieut Shaw and find him dying. One of the noblest men I ever knew. We visit Lieut. Grier.

July 19th— Walk to Camp Winder Hospital. Ride to camp and find J. J. Wicker dead. Spend night in camp.

July 20th — Preach and visit sick. Ride to Pa's late.

July 21 — Ride to camp with wife and children and find Capt. D. C. Allen, Lieutenant Cain, Sergeant Ellis and many others sick. In the afternoon visit Leonard, Galloway, Grier, etc.

July 22 — Ride to Mechanicsville with wife and children. Visit battlefield. Bury A. D. McPherson.

July 23 — Visit Grier. Last visit. He dies on 26th. Get permission to go to North Carolina with sick child.

July 24 — Leave Richmond at 4 a. m. and reach Wilmington at 8 p. m. Spend night at Mrs. McCaleb's Hotel.

July 25 — Steamer *North Carolina* takes us to White Hall.

Sunday, 27 — Visit Sunday School at Bladen Springs. Capt. John Barr Andrews died at Richmond, Virginia, July 23, 1862. He was the first person to whom I spoke after I found peace with God, Oct. 15, 1853, at University of North Carolina.

July 28— Spend day with Bro. W. A. Savage. Meet Rev. D. C. Johnson, his pastor.

July 29 — Ride to Elizabethtown. Wife spends day with old Mrs. McKay on her farm. Spend the night with Mr. Russ.

July 31, 1862 — Wife and children ride with me to White Hall. Part with loved ones, to meet _____?

Aug. 1, 1862, A. M.— In Wilmington. Blue! Blue! Leave for Richmond at 2 p. m., taking a lot of vegetables for S. T. Buie & Bro., 18th North Carolina Regiment.

Aug. 2 — Miss connection at Petersburg. Get to Richmond at 6 p. m. and hear that Lieutenant Cain is about to die in Camp Winder Hospital.

Sunday, Aug. 3, 1862 — Preach in the morning. Hear that Lieut, Cain died at 9 a. m. and Lieut. Pitt about to die. Ride anxiously to Hospital, and find Pitt died at 5 p. m. Return to Richmond sad at 9 p. m.

Aug. 4th— Spend afternoon visiting my sick at Winder. Look at Lieutenant Cain and Pitt for the last time. Dine at Pa's. Write to Mary. Visit

Brother Amos and wife, Leonard and Lieut. Galloway, and reach camp late.

Aug. 5 —Visit Rev. H. G. Hill, Chaplain 13th Regiment. Meet Rev. J. Rumple of Salisbury and Rev. Van Eaton. Hear Rumple conclude his sermon, and Van Eaton through all of his. Good feeling among soldiers.

Aug. 6 —Visit all my sick at Division Hospital. Thence to Richmond. Visit Samuel Wescott and Rev. W. C. Power, Chaplain 14th Regiment, sick. Visit my many sick at Winder. Some will die. Return late to camp.

Aug. 7— Fever all day. May the Lord restore me soon so that I may administer to others.

Aug. 8 — Ride early to Pa's calling at three Hospitals. Fever all day. Take medicine at night.

Aug. 8— Go late and walk to camp.

Sunday, Aug. 10— Hear Rev. Rumple preach to 4th Regiment. A poor stranger mustered in this day as a substitute for Reams of Company "G." dies very suddenly. He called himself Wayne, from Alexandria, hut a discharge for Williams was found in his pocket. Mysterious and sad! Brother Rumble preached a good sermon for me at night.

Aug. 13 — Visit sick at Division and Winder Hospital. Lieutenants Davis, Jackson and Johnson, and privates Jackson, Jenkins, Hester and Merritt doing well. Marshall Teachy will hardly live. Lieutenant McLeod hardly can recover. Peter Stanley out of his head, imagines himself on Lockwood's Folly. Says he has seen his wife and children! Perhaps he has. Prays right intelligently. Poor old Mr. Graham will hardly go in ranks again. My private roll says: Samuel W. Graham, born in Ireland, was living in Chatham County, North Carolina, when he enlisted in Company "H" September 23, 1861, was forty-six years old and left two motherless children. He died next day. Scotland and Ireland furnished several good soldiers to that company. Dennis Carr and Andrew McFarland were born in Ireland. James Rogers, William McCulloch and A. D. McGill were born in Scotland. McCulloch was thirty-seven when he enlisted, and left two motherless children when he was lost, or reported "missing;" McGill was nineteen. He has lived to be a blessing to North Carolina. He has been heard in the halls of her Legislature. Graham seemed to know me the day before he died. Teachy called me "Brother Betts," as usual though he had recognized no one for some days. Died August 14, 1862, leaving a wife and five children. After supper I call to see Revs. L. and B. Culbreth, A. Maxwell and D. Ray at Hotel. (Love and Blackman Culbreth were brothers, local preachers, raised in Sampson County, North Carolina. Blackman died early. Love, a sweet singer and a fine preacher, had given a son to the

Experience of a Confederate Chaplain 1861–1865

North Carolina Conference in 1859, and lived till 1896.) Return to Pa's by moonlight, praying and meditating, and receive a blessing on my soul.

Aug. 14th — Go to Female Institute Hospital and find no entry of the name of my Brother Grier, who died there during my visit to North Carolina. Find his valise, etc. Will send his brother for it. Col. May, of Georgia, says Brother Grier died between midnight and day, July 26, no one knowing when he died. Holy angels knew.

Aug. 15 — Ride to see Regimental Work Squad with Chaplains Long, Moore and Hill.

Aug. 16 — Morning in camp. Supper in Richmond, and return and hear Brother J. G. Barkley preach. (This dear man raised his children in Nash county, North Carolina, and lived to be very old. Died April 16, 1896. He said to me in his house in 1887 or 1888: "Brother Betts, the happiest day in my life was one day in 1840, when I saw my oldest daughter marry a young man and start to Africa! Glory to God for such religion!"

Sunday, Aug. 17 — Brother Barkley preaches in morning and I in evening. Receive marching orders.

Aug. 19 — Rise at 4 with orders to march to Gordonsville. Leave some sick in camp. Others, not able to march, start and have to fall out. Division passes through Richmond. I stop and buy flannel and overtake regiment six and one-half miles out. Sleep on ground.

Aug. 20— Rise at 4 and march. Night at Taylorsville. At 10 at night brigade called to arms and marched off — weary, weary. I remain on the ground praying for our soldiers.

Aug. 21 — Threatened with jaundice. Take medicine.

Aug. 24 — Dark and damp. One year ago today, my dear little Eddie was cold in death in parsonage in Smithville (Southport), North Carolina, and I was almost dead. I preached on "Samaritan."

August 25, 1862 — My birthday! Thirty years old! And yet how little knowledge I have acquired! How little grace! How little good have I done! God help me in time to come! Get marching orders at nine at night.

Aug. 26 — Long hard march on our men.

Aug. 29 — Called at C. H. and wrote to wife. Camped at Rapidan. I slept under a wagon.

Aug. 30 — Men wade Rapidan, and I drink of it. Pass Cedar Run, where there had been a hard fight August 9. Robert Henderson, a venerable old man, had been arrested. As our men passed his gate he said with tears, "God preserve you, my boys!" Pass Culpepper C. H. Town and country around desolated by war. Sick and wounded Federals in town.

Aug. 31 — It began to rain before day. Just then we received orders,

"Be ready to move at a moments' warning." We needed rest, and were hoping we could enjoy that Sabbath in the woods. As I leaped from my blanket and started to find my horse, I began to sing, not knowing what. As I heard "Happy people over yonder, where they rest forever more," my heart melted with joy. I was then a "happy" man. (The thirty-four years and nineteen days since that dark morning have brought me nearer to the "happy people over yonder" and greatly increased their number.) March all day. Muddy to "Muddy Run." Pass Warrenton, Sulphur Springs, lovely, blighted village.

September 1, 1862 — Pass Warrenton. Rainy, cold night.

Sept. 2 — Pass down to Groveton, where fearful fighting was done last week, August 28, 29 and 30. Horrid scenes! Many dead Federals still on the field, though a squad of their men, under flag of truce, has been some days caring for wounded and burying dead.

I found a wounded Federal sitting on the field — a broken thigh, a rifle ball through his arm and a bruised shoulder made him right helpless. His undressed wounds were sore. He asked me if I thought our surgeons would care for him. I assured him they would. He said he had a wife and two little children in his northern home. His parents were pious and had raised him piously, but he had neglected his own soul, I said: "Brother, Jesus loves you. You came down here to kill my brothers, but I love you." He broke down and sobbed aloud: "You don't talk like one man that came here. He upbraided me." He told me our men had been very good to him during the three or four days he had been there. As one hurried by he would give him water and food, and raise him up to rest certain tired muscles. Another would stop to give him more food and water and lay him down.

They had just taken the last Confederate wounded from that part of the field. He was on the surgeon's table a few yards away. I trust this Federal was soon taken to that table. As I was about to hurry away to overtake my regiment he asked me to lay him down! How could I? Where could I take hold? I did the best I could. As I took him by the hand and commended him to God, I think my heart was as tender as it ever was. His bones may be in that field now. I hope to meet his soul in Heaven in a few years. Hurry on ten miles and overtake our regiment. Sleep cold and take cold. Frost next morning.

Sep. 3, 1862 — Pass Leesburg. Call at a farm house to buy corn. A Union woman upbraids me. See Sugar Loaf Mountain in Maryland.

Sep. 4 — Dine with Mrs. Sanders in Leesburg. She is the mother-in-law of Rev. W. G. Cross.

Sep. 5 — March all day. Call and buy eggs and butter from a man in Morrisonville, for which he would receive no pay.

September 6 — Turn and march down the river, and camp near Cheek's Ford.

Sunday, Sep. 7 — Cross Potomac while the bands are playing *Maryland! My Maryland!* Some cross the River of Death next Sunday.

Sep. 9 — Ride to Frederick City and return. Its population is 9,000 or 10,000.

Sep. 10 — Whole army in motion. Dine at Mr. Fitzhugh's in Frederick City. Lovely family. Mr. Jones, next door. Meet Rev. Auguste, Chaplain 15th Virginia Regiment, Joseph Shawen, a good Southern Methodist, Col. Henson, President of the County Bank, aged and venerable (but had been arrested by the Federals), and Rev. Mr. Ross, a Presbyterian. Spend the night with Colonel Carmack in Frederick City. Strong Southern feeling among these good people.

Sep. 11, 1862 — Having been very feeble for two or three days I spend a day at Colonel Carmack's. Brigade passed at 8 a. m. At 2:30 I go on and stop at Boonsboro with Dr Josiah Smith. Strong intelligent Southern feeling.

Sep. 14 — Our Brigade goes out at 4:30 a. m. My horse being lame, I cannot go. General Garland is brought to his tent dead. I go to see him. A few days ago I saw him under different circumstances that will make me admire him forever. His Brigade was crossing a stream on a narrow footway. His men began to plunge into the little stream, up to their knees. He knew it would be bad for them to march with wet feet. He drew up his fiery horse in the road in the water and stayed there till his entire command had passed, pointing to the narrow bridge and shouting to the men, compelling them to take time and go over in single file. That manly form now lies before me silent but "speaking." Hear Captain Wicker is wounded. At midnight wagons move circuitously to Williamsport. I start to my regiment and find everybody moving silently. Coming near Boonsboro, I feel lonely as I see not a form on the pike. Enter town and see Division after Division passing toward the west.

Monday, Sep. 15, 1862 — Regiment rest in field at 7 a. m. They need rest. Yesterday was a busy day and last night gave us rest. Cross Antietam Creek and make a stand on hill adjacent. An occasional artillery shot occupies the evening. Men in arms. I spent night with ambulances on vacant lot in Sharpsburg.

Sep. 16 — Artillery begins at 8:30 a. m. After 11 firing ceases. We move our Brigade Hospital two miles in the rear.

Sep. 17 — Very heavy firing in morning. Wounded coming in. God help our men to fight! Have mercy on those who are to die! At noon Colonel Parker and Adjutant Phillips come wounded. A rifle ball passed over Colonel Parker's head, cutting away a narrow strip of skin and plowing a nice little furrow in the skull, leaving the membrane that covers the brain visible but uninjured. What a narrow escape! Fierce contest all day. Lieutenant Rogers killed (Co. D), Sergeant Edwards killed (Co. C), Colonel Tew, of 2nd Regiment, was killed also. Lieut. Duncan E. McNair, of Robeson, my classmate for many years, was killed, leaving a wife and child. Our regiment lost a number of brave men at Sharpsburg; some killed, others mortally wounded.

Sep. 18 — No fighting. I visit Colonel Parker and ride over to Sharpsburg and see how the town had been shelled. Rainy, damp night. Wake up at midnight and find everything moving to the rear.

Sep. 19 — Before day we drink our coffee and ride to the Potomac, leaving Drs. Gregory and Lawson and a few wounded and sick. Though troops and wagons have been passing all night, still the roads and fields were full. Ram! Jam! Wagons and ambulances turned over! One man was killed by the overturning of an ambulance. Cross at daybreak. Yesterday I bathed in this stream. Today dead bodies will be bathing in it. Pass three miles back to division wagon train and stop to rest. Shelling begins on river at 9:30 a. m. Division moves in afternoon and spends night one and a half miles west of Shepardstown. See Captain Baskerville going home, and write to wife.

Sep. 20 — Fierce cannonading from 10 to 11. Still as death from 1 to 2. While troops are in line of battle I visit five wounded men at house of William Goldenbanger. Col. W. J. McGill lost his left arm. He has a wife and three children. Trusts in God. John C. McMahon, of Mississippi, Caohoma county, was with Walker in Nicaragua, passed safely many perils in many places, and was wounded in the arm and side at Sharpsburg, and at last turned over in the ambulance in which the man was killed two days ago. He is well bred and polite and confesses his sinfulness. Did he ever get back to his native home and see his venerable father, Rev. Wm. McMahon?

Sep. 21 — Hear Rev. A. A. Watson, chaplain 2nd Regiment, preach. Write to Mary by Mr. Van Bokelin.

Sep. 22— Ride to the wagons to rest. Five years ago this afternoon my second son, Willie, was born. God bless him and spare us to see each other. Ride to Martinsburg in afternoon. Lie beside my horse at night, gazing at the stars and thinking of Mary and my little ones. "What is man, that

Thou art mindful of him?"

Sep. 23— Visit 18th and 28th Regiments.

Sep. 25 — Dine with Harry Thomas, near Martinsburg, a thrifty farmer, fine-looking, genial gentleman. I met Mr. Thomas afterwards in another section and greeted him as such. He looked at me as if he did not remember me. I gave him my name and said: "Is this Mr. Harry Thomas?" He said: "No, it is his brother Jack." I told him I had met his brother and was glad to meet him. Some time after I met Mr. Thomas and called him Thomas. He evidently did not remember me. I quickly asked him if he was Mr. Harry or Jack. He said it was neither, but their brother Jake! I wish I could see the three together.

Sunday, Sep. 28, 1862 — Preach in camp.

Sep. 29 — Ride to Winchester with sick men. Meet Captain Drake and Captain Witherspoon on road with mail. Get letter from wife. Little Mary quite ill on 12th. May now be in Heaven. Father, into thy hands. I commend my child. Stop with Rev. W, G. Eggleston, P. E. of this District of the Baltimore Conference. Lately lost his wife. Has a family of children.

Sep. 30. — Ride to camp and carry Brigade mail. Meet Rev. J. A. Robbins, a schoolmate, now from Georgia.

October 1, 1862 — Carry sundry letters to their places. Receive pay for July and August.

Oct. 3 — Hear from wife, at Chapel Hill. Babe is better. She went from Bladen to Chapel Hill with three children and a nurse (about one hundred miles) by private conveyance.

Sunday, Oct. 5— Preach to a large, attentive audience. Fine day. Bright night.

Oct. 6 — Pay Captain Allen my mess bill for May, June and July.

Oct. 7 — Ride to Winchester in ambulance with the sick. Visit E. Fletcher Bobbitt at Academy Hospital. Last interview with a lovely man. Brother of Rev. Drs. W. H. and J. B. Bobbitt of the North Carolina Conference. Left his family in Warren county. Joined army in May '62, and died in Richmond, October 23, 1862. Roster says 1863; but my book is right. I never can forget how tenderly he spoke of his wife, saying he did not know how to appreciate her till the war took him from her. Carry Rev. Vaughn, chaplain of 3rd Regiment, to camp.

Oct. 8— Walk five miles with J. W. Ellis as he starts to North Carolina as Senator. This Christian gentleman, a lawyer of Columbus county, enlisted in Co. E as a private, August 28, 1861. His friends elected him to the North Carolina Senate in 1862. He had a walk of about ninety miles to Staunton, the railroad track having been torn up. I put his knapsack on my horse and claimed the pleasure of walking a few miles with him.

Oct. 12 — Preach in morning. Captain Atwell died at Shepardstown.

Oct. 14 — Tiresome ride to Shepardstown to see wounded men, Hathaway, Brown, Dement and Lieutenant Crews. A minie ball passed through his chest at Sharpsburg. (I had no idea he could live; but in 1870 and 1871 I was his pastor at Oxford.) Spend night at Hon. Alex. Boteler's. Go to see Captain Osborn at Shepardstown. Among the brave men left at Shepardstown, too badly wounded at Sharpsburg to be taken any distance, was Col. W. L. DeRossett, of Wilmington, North Carolina. I there first met him and his venerable father, Dr. A. J. DeRossett. (The Colonel lived a cripple for life, was largely useful, and raised an interesting family. The father lived to extreme old age and died in 1897.) Get Lieutenant Harrell's sword. George K. Harrell was wounded at Sharpsburg, but returned to duty and carried that sword till he was killed, May 12, 1864. See Colonel McGill at house of Dr. Lucas, two and a half miles out. His wife is with him.

Oct. 17 — Ready to march before day. Rev. Power, of 14th Regiment, arrives.

Oct. 19 — Preach to a small congregation. Major General D. H. Hill a devout hearer. A. R. McDonald, of Moore county arrives, and spends night with me.

Oct. 21 — Captain Witherspoon and I ride to Winchester. He meets Mrs. R. H. Apperson at hotel in trouble. She rides in ambulance to near Whitehall, and thence on saddle to Mr. Zephaniah Silver's and finds her husband convalescent. Happy soldier! Happy wife! Silver family so nice and kind. Two sons in our army.

Oct. 22 — Ride with Captain Apperson to our camp. Bury Sergeant Cornelius Savage of Company E.

Oct. 24 — Fail to get clothing which I much need. Get marching orders.

Oct. 25 — Division moves and begins to tear up track of W and Harper's Ferry R. R. Our Brigade operates on track below Charlestown during the night in a cold rain.

Sunday, Oct. 26 — Cool rain. Sit till noon under tent in front of fire. Brigades of troops passing to and fro through rain. Men suffer. Very cool rain and wind all night. Large fire in front of tent all night.

Oct. 27 — Brigade goes off to tear up railroad track. Revs. Power, Long and I go to Charlestown and ride on the spot of John Brown's execution, and see the prison in which he was confined. Lovely little town.

Oct. 31, 1862 — Cross Shenandoah river at Berry's Ferry. Men wade.

Cross mountain at Ashby's Gap.

Nov. 1 — Bro. Power and I walk up the mountain and spend two or three hours. Fine view. Pray together up there.

Nov. 2 — Bro. Power begins to preach at 10:30, but troops are ordered out and fall back toward Paris and lie in line of battle all night.

Nov. 5 — Brigade in camp near Fort Royal. Call on Rev. Dr. Hough, pastor of M. E. Church, South. Lovely man and wife.

Nov. 6 — Hoarse and feeble. Bad cold. Move across river after night. Very cold. Men wade and walk a mile to camp, some without shoes. Water freezes by my side as I lie on the ground.

Nov. 7 — Snow begins to fall at 10 a. m, Bad day on bare feet.

Nov. 8 — General Hill calls for volunteers to render daring, dangerous service for two or three days. We have prayers at our fire.

Nov. 9 — Division moves to Strasburg. Barefoot men march in snow. Bury H. Y. Kirkpatrick at night in Presbyterian cemetery. He enlisted at nineteen, from Mecklenburg county. Lovely Christian. Died in the house of Mrs. Davis, November 8th, 10:30 p. m. How sad the sight! How tenderly a few of his comrades raked away the snow, dug the grave and laid the noble youth away! The chaplain's prayer is that he and they may meet him on the Resurrection Day.

Nov. 11 — Brigade moves six or seven miles and tears up railroad track at night.

Nov. 12 — Hear Bro. Moore preach in his camp.

Nov. 13 — Bro. Power and I ride to Strasburg and visit hospitals, and see Robt. L. White die. A Christian. New Testament in his bosom.

Nov. 14 — Visit sick at hospitals in Strasburg.

Nov. 15 — I walk out to study my Bible. Wash day in 2nd Regiment. Bank of branch lined some distance with men half naked, some washing pants and drawers, others washing shirts and some picking their clothing. Some half naked holding their wet clothes to the fire to dry. Sad sight! Would make wives, mothers and sisters weep.

Sunday, Nov. 16 — Inspection in morning. I preach in afternoon, and Bro. Power and I deliver the Holy Communion to twenty persons. At night Dr. Garrett and Dr. Smith, who could not be present in the afternoon, receive it in my tent, Dean, a negro servant, also.

Nov. 17 — Division moves and camps six miles from Strasburg. Visit sick at hospitals, one man dying, no one knows who or where from.

GETTING A FURLOUGH

Nov. 18 — As my Conference was to meet in Raleigh December 3, 1 had made application for leave of absence and my furlough had not come. So I get duplicate and take it to officers myself. Leave General Hill at 2:45 p.m., ride ten and a half miles to General Jackson's headquarters, get my paper signed, return late. My first papers came to hand ten or twenty minutes after I left.

Nov. 19 — In camp. Moses Ezzell very ill. Prayer meeting at night.

GETTING HOME! FIVE DAYS!

Nov. 20 — Six miles on saddle, twelve on wagon, five on foot.

Nov. 21 — Wagon and ambulance to Mt. Crawford. Spend night in Baptist church with fifty or sixty sick men. Pray with them. All seem to feel. Many happy. Almost all of them Christians.

Nov. 22 — Take stage at 3 a. m. Pass Willow Pump — a curiosity. Some one had planted a willow post near a gate on the roadside to discharge the T water from an underground pipe, the willow sprouted, made quite a tree and still discharged the water. Such a blessing to thirsty soldiers. Take cars to Staunton and reach Richmond.

Nov. 23 — Miss Wilmington train at Weldon and go on to Raleigh. Hear sermon at M. E. Church and greet several friends warmly. Call on Mrs. Seaton Gales and pay her $250 from her husband. Lovely woman. Children all sick with scarlet fever, and her husband far away, Sleep on parlor floor in W. T. Bain's hotel.

Nov. 24 — Pass Goldsboro and Wilmington. Leave cars at Brinkley's. Walk to Dr. Buie's. He gives me buggy to Capt. Jo. Green's. He gives me a good horse and saddle to D. D. Allen's.

Nov. 25 — Bro. Allen sends me in buggy, and I see my family once more. All well. Thank God! Fever from vaccination makes me delirious during night. Had not seen family since July 31. In going home from the army I met Lieut. E. Ruark, of Co. C. on his way home at Smithville, on sick furlough. We sat together for many, many miles, and parted at Wilmington. He went home and died of smallpox, spreading it and killing his mother and others. Narrow escape for me and mine. Neither of us thought of the danger.

Nov. 29 — Preach at Bladen Springs.

GETTING TO CONFERENCE

Dec. 3, 1862 — Start to Raleigh, about ninety miles, taking wife, three children and a nurse. Rain all day. Spend night with Bro. Sykes.

Dec. 4 — Pass Fayetteville. Spend night with J. H. Hawley, one of the best men I ever knew.

Dec. 5 — Rain all day. Spend night with Allen Betts, my brother.

Dec. 6 — Clear and cold. Ride to Alvin Betts, my brother.

Dec. 7 — Hear Bishop Early preach in Raleigh.

Dec. 8 — Day in Conference. A letter from Uncle Foster Utley, Chapel Hill, leads me to send my family to that place.

Dec. 9 — Send family on cars to Chapel Hill, while I turn my face towards Bladen alone. After four days of lonely riding I reach my wife's boarding place and pack books and clothes, and take Steamer *Hurt* for Fayetteville. Pay Jo. Russ ten dollars to take my carriage to Fayetteville.

Dec. 13 — Meet James Marley Smith, and go with him to his farm.

Sunday, Dec. 14 — Hear Bro. J. D. Buie preach at Fayetteville. Night at hotel. I have had fever for last three days.

Dec. 15 — Take cars to Egypt. Find no horse there for me. Walk about ten miles, and ride on a mule-cart about the same distance and reach Pittsboro. Sup with John Womach. He sends me to Chapel Hill, eighteen miles, on a mule-cart. Get there at 7 a. m.

Dec. 17— Chill at night.

Dec. 18— Chill in the afternoon. In bed till 22nd.

Sunday, Dec. 28— Preach in M. E. Church.

1863. THANK GOD!

Cut wood two or three days. Hard work.

Rev. J. W. Jenkins arrives on Saturday, Jan. 3. I attend Masonic meeting.

Jan. 4 — Hear Bro. Jenkins preach in morning. Spend afternoon reading my Greek Testament.

Jan. 5— Get ready to start to Virginia. At eleven at night I leave, the moon shining bright, but my spirits being sad. Luter takes me to Durham.

Jan. 6 — Reach Raleigh and draw pay for November and December, 1862. Night at Bain's Hotel.

Jan. 7 — Leave Raleigh at day. Meet Rev. M. J. Hunt and Dr. Smith on train. Meet Dr. J. S. Robinson on his way to Virginia. Miss train at Petersburg. Spend night with my cousin, Grey Utley, of Chapel Hill, at his boarding house.

Jan. 8 — Reach Richmond and find Lieuts. Carr and Swain sick there.

Jan. 9 — Snow on ground. Capt. Collins and I go on to Guinea Station, and thence to our regiment. Meet Rev. F. M. Kennedy, of the South Carolina Conference, on his way to report for duty as Chaplain for 28th North Carolina Regiment, now in General Lee's army.

Sun. Jan. 11 — Preach twice. Damp, cold weather. Sleeping on ground gives me bad cold.

Jan. 16 — J. B. Williams, of Co. "C," dies at 6 a. m., suddenly. Bury him. at 6 p. m. Turns very cold. Slept in a dark barn last night. Where tonight? In a wagon.

Sun. 18 — Preach in cold wind.

Jan. 19 — Go to Richmond. Too late for express. I mail official papers to Raleigh for Capt. Collins.

Jan. 20 — Busy all day. Buy some things for Regiment. Visit Congress. Write to wife.

Jan. 21 — Visit Richard Lloyd. Rain. Fall on box and bruise right thigh. Fire at night. Fall in street and bruise left knee badly.

Jan. 22 — Ship sundry boxes to Regiment. Quite lame from yesterday's falls.

Jan. 23 — Leave early for Guinea. Reach camp late. Mud! Mud!

Jan. 24, 1862 — Met Rev. J. W. Ward, Missionary Baptist, 3rd Va. Infantry; Rev. W. E. Walters, Jenkins S. C. Brigade.

Sunday Jan. 25. — Hear Bro. Barkley of Nash county, N. C. preach to my regiment in a. m., Bro. Power in p. m., and at wagon yard at night.

Jan. 26 — Ride to Division Surgeon for W. H. Westcott of Smithville. That must have been the last I saw of that noble boy. He was dying of chronic diarrhea. He got as far as Wilmington, where he died Feb. 28, 1864. His good father and mother were my friends. Glad I put up my tent on 26, for it snows all day on 28.

Jan. 29 — Men very cheerful, though the snow is nearly knee deep.

Sunday February 1 — Preach in camp. Visit our regiment on picket about three miles away. Rain at night.

February 2 — Seven years ago! My first son, Henry Watson, was born in Mrs. Meade's Hotel, Martinsville, Va. That morning I knelt silently upon the floor in my wife's room and prayed and wept when I first felt parental responsibility. God bless my boy today! Seven years old! May he spend many useful, happy years on earth and get safe to Heaven! God bless the mother today, and Willie and Mamie. My dear sainted Eddie! Safe in Heaven! Your father hopes to embrace you by-and-by in your angel home. Wrote to wife and Mrs. Meade.

Feb. 3 — Exceedingly cold.

Feb. 4 — Still very cold. Freezes my ink

Feb. 5 — Snow begins falling early and falls steadily.

Feb. 6 — Ride four miles in rain, hunting a cabin for Jack Faircloth, Co. A., who is very sick and weak. He will die.

Feb. 7 — Send to Gen. Rodes for brigade to be allowed to go to church on Sunday.

Feb. 8 — Bright day. Preach to a large, attentive congregation in Baptist church. Bros. Power and Thigpen assist in communion. Precious season! Hear from wife and Bro. Hunt.

Feb. 9 — Much indisposed.

Feb. 10 — Visit Brigade Hospital established yesterday. Pray with patients and Dr. Guffy. Poor Faircloth says he loves Jesus because He loved him. I, this morning, finished my fifth annual reading through the Bible. On Sampson Circuit, 1857, I went the first time regularly through this Holy Book. I hope to read it carefully through every year of my future life. Jack Faircloth dies at night. Bad night with my cough.

Feb. 11 — Rainy. Bury Faircloth. Finish Matthew in Greek.

Feb. 12 — Right unwell. Visit Hospital.

Feb. 13 — Indisposed. A. Crisp, Co. F., dies at midnight.

Feb. 14 — Bury Crisp. A. Mitchel, Co. A., dies at 3 p. m.

Feb. 15 — Rainy. Ed Register, Co. A., dies at Brigade Hospital.

Feb. 16 — Ride to Medical Board with some sick men. Get them off to hospital. Bury Ed Register.

Feb. 17 — Ground covered with snow and still it comes. Saw enemy's balloon yesterday. Not today.

Feb. 18 — Rains gently all day. I walk to new camp through rain and mud.

Feb. 19 — Pray with regiment.

Feb. 20 — Regiment goes on picket just below Fredericksburg. Ride to Fredericksburg. Call at store house of Arthur Bernard. Sad destruction of his property. He has not been seen since the enemy took him in Dec. Fine paintings in one room, "Hope and Memory," "Cleopatra," etc. Call on Bro. Owen, Chaplain 17th Mississippi Regiment. Meet Rev. Dr. Stiles at sister Fitzgerald's. Night in camp.

Feb. 22 — Rise at six, and find snow a foot deep. Snows nearly all day. Sit in my tent and read and write. Hear many heavy guns just at 12. Washington's Birthday.

Feb. 24 — Regiment, relieved from picket, comes into camp.

Feb. 26 — Prayer meeting in Co. I. Chill and fever at night.

Feb. 27— In bed.

Feb. 28 — Bro. Owen, 17 Mississippi Regiment, calls on me. Dr. Stiles and he still blessed in Fredericksburg with revival power.

March 2, 1863 — Take train and reach Richmond. See bloody coffin on cars. Deserter!

March 3 — Reach Chapel Hill, N. C, sick and tired, but find family well.

March 5 — Ride to Jehiel Atwater's and some other places.

March 8 — Preach in M. E. Church. Hear Bro. Jenkins preach Mrs. Husky's funeral at night.

March 9 — Plant Irish potatoes.

March 11 — Attend and pray at college prayers at University of N. C. Buy corn.

March 12 — At 9 P. M., start to my regiment. Hard to part with family under such circumstances. Muddy ride to Durham. No seat to Raleigh! No seat to Weldon! Trains all miss connection at Weldon. Delay seven hours there.

March 14 — Reach Richmond thirty-four and a half hours after leaving Chapel Hill. Standing all the way on trains. Walk to Winder Hospital. Thence to Seabrook Hospital. Call on Gen. Winder for Mrs. H. & B.

March 15 — Dark, damp and cool. Reach regiment 1½ miles from Hamilton's Crossing. Hail storm in afternoon

March 16 — Meet chaplains of the 2nd corps at Baptist church near Division Headquarters. Pleasant meeting. Rev. B. T. Lacy will be of great service to us. Only forty-four chaplains in corps. Without chaplains, forty-seven regiments and battalions, besides artillery.

March 17 — In camp. Bury Fraley, of Second N. C. Regiment. Build chimney to my tent. Prayer meeting in Co. E.

March 18 — Prayers in camp.

March 20— Snow! Snow!

March 21 — Very wet.

March 22 — Clear in p. m. I read to our Regiment the address of Dr. Ford to the Army of the Southwest.

March 24 — Meet chaplains of this corps at Round Oak church. Am made chairman and elected to preach to them at next meeting. Thus meeting, talking, planning and praying, we find great help for our work.

March 25 — Write to Bishop Atkinson, Dr. Mott, Bro. J. C. Brent and N. C. Presbyterian. Prayer meeting every night in some company of my Regiment. Considerable religious interest.

March 26 — Prepare sermon for Friday.

March 27 — Fine day. Fast and pray. Preach to Thirtieth and Second Regiments in our camp. Attention good. Day well observed.

March 28 — Rain all day. Finish writing to churches for Co. G. Note: I talked with each church member in each company about his spiritual condition as often as I could. Once a year I wrote home to each church about its members and sent any message anyone wanted to send, and asked the church at home to pray for us. This was expensive, laborious work, but it was for souls whom Jesus died to save. I trust many soldiers and many members at home were benefited by the labor. About 11 years after the war I met Rev. Paul Smith, a local preacher, near Mt. Pleasant. He told me he had a letter from me during the war. I told him I had no re-collection of having written to him. He said he was class leader at Cold Spring church in those days, and my letter was about old Bro. Hagler. The *Roster of N. C. Troops* says he enlisted from Sampson County Sept. 12, 1863. I cannot blame the editor of the roster for a mistake once in a while. He had so many thousands of names and dates, the wonder is that he made so few mistakes. Bro. Hagler was from Cabarrus county, 44 years old and left a wife and six children. The *Roster* gives no account of his death. He fell dead suddenly near Spottsylvania Court House May 1864. He was a good man and I loved him. The reader must imagine my feelings when I found I was the pastor of John Hagler's wife and children. Glad and sad was my heart every time I visited them.

March 29 — Very rainy, could not preach.

March 30 — Snow, hail and rain.

March 31 — Rain and hail all a. m.

April 3 — Prayer meeting every night.

April 4 — Fierce wind all day. Hard on soldiers. Dr. Grissom gets to camp. Hear from Rev. Mr. Sherwood. Snow all night.

April 5 — Snow all a. m. Sore throat.

April 6 — Visit G. T. Swain, Co. C, near camp, quite sick.

April 7 — Meet chaplains of this corps. Preach to them and many others. Good meeting. All day with them. Such meetings warm the heart and encourage us.

April 8 — In camp busy writing to the officers of thirteen regiments asking them if they wish our next conference to send them chaplains. Lieut. Ellis goes to work to raise money to buy a horse for his chaplain. Col P. gives twenty dollars, others smaller sums.

April 9 — My application for leave of absence, to be with my wife during "an important crisis" returns "disapproved!" It was approved by regiment, brigade and division commanders but "disapproved" by corps commander, T. J. Jackson. I felt no bitterness toward him, as he was conscientious. I think he had never seen his only child, Julia. He set great store on the presence and services of chaplains among the soldiers. He knew the campaign would soon open, and he wanted chaplains to be on hand to care for the wounded and dying. He and others must trust their wives in God's hands and he thought chaplains ought.

"Respectfully forwarded disapproved, T. J. Jackson." Whatever "Stonewall" disapproved we might expect Gen. Lee to disapprove. My heart sank within me when I read the short, last entry: "Respectfully returned disapproved by order of Gen. R. E. Lee." My diary gives some of the cries of my heart in that sad hour.

April 10 — Procured subscribers for sundry religious papers and forwarded $73.50 for them. Wrote to wife. Met Rev. Bennick, of S. C. Conference, chaplain 24th N. C. Regiment, Bro. Marshall, 12th Georgia Regiment, conducts morning prayers for me. Get bundle *N. C. Christian Advocates*. The paper is revived, thank God! Get letters from Rev. M. Miller and Rev. J. J. Lansdell. Write to Rev. W. E. Pell.

April 12 — I kept a little volume in my bosom, giving a verse of scripture for each day in the year. The verse for April 12 was Matt. 26, 42: "Oh, my Father, if this cup may not pass away from me, except I drink it, Thy will be done." By his help I said: "Thy will be done," and went on happy in my work. Bro J. Win. Jones, 13th Va. and Dr. Curtis, 57th N. C. Regiments arrive. Bro. Jones preaches for me. Dine and walk to Bro. Jones' regiment and preach. After supper I walk alone by Hamilton's Crossing to camp. Letter from Bishop Atkinson.

April 13 — In camp. Visit Geo. T. Swain at Younge's.

April 14 — Meet chaplains. Rev. Brigadier General Pendleton, D. D., was with us. Bro. Nelson preaches. Happy meeting. Chaplains agree to pray for each other at sunset every day.

April 15 — Rainy day. Oh, Mary, I expected to start to you today!

April 16— Write to Mary. Visit 20th and 12th Regiments.

April 17 — Walk to Hamilton's Crossing to get telegram from wife. Buy twenty-four Testaments. Bro. Jones walks back to 60th Georgia Regiment with me.

April 18- — Chaplains Patterson and Smith at prayers with us. I preach to Gordon's Brigade. Bro. Lacy preaches in p. m.

Sun, 19 — Prayers early. Preach at 10 a. m. Get telegram. "I am well," from wife. Thank God! Oh, Father, be with her! Preach in 2nd Regiment in p. m. Prayer meeting in Co. "G," at night. Decided interest.

Apr. 20 — Rain all day. Public service at 10. Read and explain Deut.

20. Get ten days furlough. Having sold my horse several months before, I was now trying to buy. Not finding a suitable one for sale, when the spring campaign, soon to open, made such demand for them, my Colonel encouraged me to apply for ten days furlough to go to North Carolina to buy one, hoping I might yet reach my wife in time to see her pass an impending crisis.

Tuesday, Apr. 21 — Damp morning. Receive two men into the church at morning prayers. Start to North Carolina.

At the beginning of the Confederate War, a chaplain was not allowed forage for a horse. I believe the U. S. Army Regulations never considered a Chaplain a mounted officer. My Colonel always drew forage for my horse as one of his. I am told that "Stonewall" Jackson asked our Congress to allow forage for each Chaplain, because he thought they could be so much more active and efficient by being mounted. My being mounted gave me a chance to help many a foot-sore, sick or wounded man. I could walk for hours and give a ride to the foot-sore or wounded. I could stop or turn aside and look after the wounded, and then hurry on and overtake my Regiment.

Apr. 23 — Get to Chapel Hill at 7 :30 a. m., and find all well.

Apr. 24 — At home.

Apr. 25 — Our fifth child, a son, is born at 3:30 a. m. Mother and child doing well. Thank God!

Apr. 26 — Hear Bro. Jenkins preach twice.

Apr. 27 — Plant corn and beans.

Apr. 28 — Buy little black mare from Charles Johnson for $200. Rain.

Apr. 29, 1863 — Over thirty-three years have passed since I wrote my diary for the above day. With a grateful heart I copy the exact words. "I wish here devoutly to acknowledge that merciful Providence that has guided me for twenty days past." I leave wife and little ones early. God blesses me at the family altar. Ride on horseback. Spend night with Mrs. M. Waller at Knap O' Reeds. Bros. Peed and Tilly called and sat with me awhile.

Apr. 30 — Meet Rev. W. C. Gannon, my Conference classmate at Tally Ho. He rides with me to Oxford. I dine with Rev. L. K. Willie. Miss my way and meet Col. C. P. Taylor. He went out as Captain of Co. "G" of 30th Regiment, but retired in May 1861. He lived and died a noble Christian. Pass Williamsboro, Townsville, and spend night with Charles Taylor.

Fri., May 1 — Cross Roanoke at Taylor's Ferry. Stop at Randolph Macon College. Meet Rev. P. W. Archer, Rev. Dr. W. A. Smith and Rev. Chipley. Pass on and spend night with Captain C. W. Bragg.

May 2 — Pass Lunenburg Court House. Meet Mrs. Ray, of Virginia Conference. Saturday night finds me with Dr. G. W. Scott. Four days in the saddle took me forty-eight miles to Oxford, thirty-six to Randolph Macon College, and fifty to Dr. Scott's.

Sun. May 3, '63 — Hear Rev. D. W. Shanks preach at Amelia Court House. He is a Presbyterian. Dine with Mr. Weising. Ride twelve miles and spend night with Mr. Smithey.

May 4 — Ride six miles to Powhattan Court House and *hear everything*. A Federal Cavalry raid had been spreading terror on the opposite side of the river. Meet Rev. Blinco of Virginia Conference. Ride twelve miles toward Jude's Ferry. Dine and go six miles further down the river by Manakin Ferry and stop with Mrs. Mosely. How excited the people! God alone can keep us quiet. Bless His name! I am in "perfect peace!"

May 5 — Ride fifteen miles to Richmond. Telegraph to Mary. Seven days in the saddle, from Chapel Hill to Richmond. Had not heard a word from my family yet. I think those had been the happiest seven days of my life up to that time. "Praising my Savior all the day long." When I knelt at sunset in the woods and prayed for the Chaplains, the soldiers, my country and my family, my soul was so happy. That telegram must have gladdened the heart of the little wife, who could not know where the husband was. She expected me to cross James River above Richmond, and did not write to me there.

May 6 — Damp and cool. Rain all day.

May 7 — Pass 11th and 52nd Regiments going to Hamilton's Crossing. Write to wife from Ashland, in the home of Rev. D. T. Wills.

May 8 — Ride over the worst roads I ever saw to old camp and find my Regiment there. Some are gone forever!

May 9 — Prayers with my men. Hear from family. Doing well, thank God!

Saturday, May 9, 1863 — Spend day among wounded. Most of the wounded of our Regiment get off on train to hospitals. Many poor strangers suffer for attention, though surgeons and nurses do all they can.

May 10 — Preach in camp. Second and Fourth regiments worship with us. General thanksgiving day for our late victory. The "victory" cost many lives. Many husbands left widows and orphans. When I made that point in my sermon, and gave number of widows and orphans left by those who fell in the 30th regiment, Gen. Grimes gave special attention, and stopped to speak to me after preaching, and said he wished he knew how many widows and orphans were left by all who fell in Lee's army in the last battle I spend p. m. among wounded at railroad. Gen. Jackson dies at 3 p. m.

May 11 — Prayers in a. m. I visit 28th Regiment and see Bro. Kennedy.

May 12 — Visit 12th, 28th, 20th and 37th Regiments.

May 13 — Wife's birthday. Yesterday, eight years ago, I married her.

May 14 — Prayer every morning and evening.

May 15 — Visit Col. Christie, of 23rd Regiment. Bro. Ervin, of South Carolina, spends night with me and preaches.

May 16 — Four new converts.

Sunday, May 17 — Preach at 9 a. m. Baptize A. S. Brown Co, H. and Alexander Co. K. Prayer meeting in p. m.

May 18 — In camp. Lieut. Orr presents me with ten dollars. Sundry other officers contribute to buy me a horse.

May 19 — Meet chaplains.

May 20 — Rev. Dr. W. J. Hoge preaches to our brigade.

May 21 — Rev. N. B. Cobb and Rev. J. A. Stradly, of North Carolina, come to Second Regiment.

May 22 — Bro. Stradly preaches for 2nd and 30th in a. m., Bro. Cobb in p. m. Prayer meeting in each at night.

May 23 — I preach to 2nd and 30th. Several converts.

May 24 — I preach twice. Baptize J. A. Underwood. Several converts. Bro. Cobb baptizes one of the 30th and four of 14th Regiments at 5 p. m.

May 25 — Examine two candidates for Missionary Baptist Church. Rev. J. H. Colton, Chaplain 53rd Regiment spends night with me. He had been my classmate three years at his father's school, Summerville, N. C, and three years at Chapel Hill.

May 26 — Meet Chaplains. Bro. Stradly preaches for me at night.

May 28 — Bro. Howard, of Sampson County, North Carolina, comes to my regiment and preaches for me. The Lord pours out His Spirit. We see twelve penitents and five converts.

May 30 — Preaching a. m. and p. m. The Lord is with us.

Sunday, May 31 — Bro. Howard preaches in a. m. and I in p. m. He immerses 8, I baptize 1 by pouring. Eleven converts in last four days.

June 1, 1863 — We continue our meeting. Bros. Cobb and Stradly helping.

June 2 — Meet chaplains. At night we see 15 penitents and several converts.

June 3 — Bro. Stradly preaches in a. m. Thirteen join the church, and two or three are converted during the meeting — 15 or 18 penitents. Army receive marching orders!

June 4 — Pass Spottslyvania Court House.

June 5 — Move on. Dr. Deems and Bros. Cobb and Stradly with us. Seven penitents at evening prayers.

June 6 — Move on. Dr. Deems preaches to our Brigade, as we rest on the road at midday. Rain. I sit under a wagon, as my tent was left. I sleep on wet leaves at night.

Sunday, June 7 — Pass Culpepper Court House. At evening worship, 29 penitents. Yesterday p. m. Bro. Cobb examined 7 candidates for his church, and I, 8 for mine.

June 8 — Dr. Deems preached for Brigade. I preach for Doles Brigade and take five into my church. Bro. Marshall, of 12th Ga., preaches for our Brigade at 6 p. m. — 28 penitents, six converts. Seven or eight join different churches.

June 9 — Dr. Deems leaves us for North Carolina, not knowing his oldest son, Theodore Disosway was to be mortally wounded at Gettysburg in a few days. March every day.

June 12 — Pass up valley and over mountain toward Front Royal. Dine with Rev. Dr. Hough and his good wife. Cross Shenandoah River.

June 13 — Pass Berryville and capture a fine deserted camp.

Sunday, June 14 — Call on Wm. Asbury, nephew of Bishop Asbury (?) Army pass on to Martinsburg. Enemy being run out, our men save some burning commissary stores.

June 15 — Cross Potomac at Williamsport and camp in Maryland. Fever in p. m. and night.

June 17 — Brigade moves to Hagerstown. I call on Oberton Homes and sup with him. Spend night with Dr. Halm at Female Seminary. He and wife so very kind.

June 19 — Leave H. at 5 p, m. Heavy rain. Ride nearly all night. Reach wagons two miles beyond Martinsburg at 5 a. m.

June 20 — Damp and dark. Retrace my steps and sleep in a barn near Hagerstown. Write wife by Bro. Stallings, Quartermaster Sergeant.

June 21 — Very unwell. Bro. Cobb preaches for our Brigade. Several are immersed in p. m.

June 22 — Division moves toward Chambersburg, Pa. Dr. J. V. Simmons in Hagerstown, fills a tooth for me and will not charge a "rebel." Enter Pennsylvania and camp near Green Castle.

June 23 — In camp. Seven penitents at night.

June 26 — Prayer meeting in J. Kenigg's barn.

June 27 — Hard march. Mud! Mud! Pass through Carlisle and camp in United States Barracks. I sleep on ground. Get two letters from wife.

Daughter sick June 4. God spare her!

Sunday, June 28 — Bro. Lacy preaches to three North Carolina Brigades in the forenoon. I preach in the afternoon and baptize five by pouring. (In 1896 I met one of them in North Carolina. He told me I baptized him at Carlisle; but I smelt whiskey on his breath in 1896.) Bro. Brooks and I baptize four each, in a pool near by. Pleasant day, but not much spirituality among the soldiers. Write to Mary at night.

June 29 — Rainy. Ride into Carlisle. Call on Marshall in College grove. Meet Rev. Dr. Johnson, President of Dickinson College. When Rev. Dr. Deems graduated there, he did not know his oldest son would hear preaching for the last time at this place and then march on to Gettysburg to be killed. Meet Rev. Grandin of Baltimore Conference, who graduated here eighteen years ago. Meet Dr. Johnson's daughter, a bright young woman, who asks me some questions. "Mr. Betts, what was your object in joining the army? "Was it to help the rebellion?" I told her I could not have taken the oath of office as Chaplain if I had not been in full sympathy with the Confederate cause, but I did not think it so weak as to need my help. I told her my love for souls led me into the work. Fixing her eyes on mine, she said: "Mr. Betts, would you be willing to see the Union restored?" I quickly said: "Miss Johnson, I would rejoice to see the Union 'restored,' but you and I will never see it 'restored.'" Visit Federal prisoners at night.

June 30 — Division crosses Blue Ridge and camp half a mile beyond Heidleburg. Dark rainy evening. I sit on a fence and write to my wife and tell her I expect to sleep on two rails on top of that fence, while soldiers sleep among the rocks around me. I add: "Thank God! I am happy." Happiness does not depend so much on our surroundings as some may think. Once I was not happy while it seems I should have been. Walking with some young people across the beautiful University grounds in North Carolina I said: "Miss Julia, it seems that a young man ought to be happy here." That expression was a confession that I was not happy. What a contrast!

July 1 —Division moves six miles by Middle Town and six and a half to Gettysburg and drive the enemy two miles. Col. Parker, Capt. C. N. Allen, Lieut. Brown and many others are wounded. Among the killed are: G. L. Swain, S. M. Hewitt, John C. Goodwin, John H. Mason and J. B. Whitley.

Col. Parker's wound was in the face. The ball entered just below one eye and came out just below the other, cutting the nasal tubes. When I knelt by him and prayed for him and his wife and children, he seemed about to strangle with the blood. I stopped praying and held my arm lovingly over him till he was quiet. He got home, returned to duty, and received another wound at Spottsylvania, and was then put on post duty. Capt. Allen's right arm was so broken up that it had to be amputated. His case will interest others. He had an idea that surgeons were fond of cutting off men's limbs. Dr. Briggs asked me to see him and try to influence him, for he refused to allow his arm amputated. Capt. Allen had lately married Miss Johns in Wake County, N. C. I prayed silently as I went to where he lay. Kneeling by him, I said, "Capt. I long for you to get home and see that lovely young wife, who is praying for you, but you will never see her if you try to keep that arm." We looked silently into each other's eyes. After a while, he said: "Mr. Betts, I wish you would call Briggs to me." I called Dr. Briggs! (Nine years after I met him in Wake. He took me to his home. Introducing me to his wife, he said, "Bro. Betts, I want to confess to you in the presence of my wife that I owe my life to you." The reader must imagine my feelings.)

July 2 — Part of the day among wounded men. Visited Brigade in town. A fearful fight from 3 till 9 p. m.

July 8 — Move hospital early. Brother Stradley and I were riding over the fields from one hospital to another, when I fell from my horse at noon, not knowing I had fallen, and remaining unconscious for an hour. Loss of sleep and excitement may have led to the vertigo. God could take a man out of this world without his knowing anything of it. Col. Bennett wounded. Lieut. Connell, of Co. G., killed.

July 4 — Move corps hospital early to a barn three miles towards Fairfield. Bury Lieut. Connell and a man of the 4th N. C. Regiment. I wrote to the young man's father, near Statesville, and told him I had buried his son. (At a Conference in Statesville, Dec. 1868, a lady called for me and told me her father, an old man too feeble to ride to town, asked her to come and find me and give his love to me, and thank me for what I had done for him. As we sat and wept, I felt a thousand times paid for my labor and my ten-cent postage stamp.) Col. Parker and Bennett start for Virginia in ambulance.

July 6 — Division moves slowly on through Fountain Dale Gap.

July 7 — Move on and camp one-and-a-half miles from Hagerstown.

July 8 — Rain and wind for five days.

July 9 — Ride to Williamsport to see our wounded.

July 10 — Day among wounded.

July 11 — Go out to Regiment in line of battle. Pray with them in the afternoon.

Experience of a Confederate Chaplain 1861–1865

July 12 — Preach to Regiment in a. m. Get three letters from Mary in p. m. All well, thank the Lord.

July 13 — Visit Regiment. Rain. Late in the afternoon start for Virginia, at twilight. Ride down through rain and mud to pontoon bridge at Falling Water. Cross at 10:30 and pass on in rain and mud to within one mile of Martinsburg. Sleep a little on two rails under a wagon. God bring our soldiers over safely!

July 14 — Ride in rain to Martinsburg, and stop with Mr. Doll. His son Dick is in 2nd Va. Regiment.

Meet Dr. Hoge. Dr. Witherspoon extracts a tooth for me.

July 15 — Spend a. m. as yesterday with sick and wounded. Army passing all day. Fever in p. m. and night. Night in field near Martinsburg.

July 16 — Very unwell. Army moves on. I stop and rest at Dr. Burkhart's in Darkville. Night in tent with Bro. Stradley. Heard from Mary. She and children are "prayerful, hopeful and happy." Got letter from Bro. Deems, inquiring after his son, Lieut. T. D. Deems, and asking me to come to see him. Dr. Deems left us for North Carolina June 9. He heard his son was wounded at Gettysburg, and had come to Winchester hoping to see or hear something of him. The military authorities did not allow citizens just then to go to our army. All he could do was to ask me to come to see him. Bro. Stradley held prayer meeting for 2nd and 20th.

July 17 — Rain, rain. Ask leave to go to "Winchester to see Dr. Deems. Colonel approves. Brigade and division commanders say there is no need for me to go! They offer to send my written statement! I meet Bro. B. T. Lacy in camp. He asks me if I have a "pass at will" from the corps commander. I tell him that is what every Chaplain ought to have. He asks me to stand still a moment. He steps into Lieutenant General's tent and returns with the needed pass. I gallop to Winchester and find Dr. Deems gone. The division commander meets me on the street. Does not ask me how I came. I wanted him to ask. I was anxious to show him my pass. It served me a good purpose many times in trying to do my duty as Chaplain in caring for sick and wounded men, and in going from point to point in that army. Colonel Christie dies.

July 18 — Ride by Mr. Silver's at White Hall. Night in camp. Peter P. Scales, my classmate at University, dies.

Sunday, July 19 — Bros. Stradley, Power and F. H. Wood, preach to our Brigade. I have prayers with my Regiment and with Dr. Sprunt, Chaplain of 20th Regiment sick.

July 22 — Carry many papers to Regiment.

July 25 — Heavy rain. Night in Mr. R's barn.

Sunday, July 26 — Preach to my Regiment in a. m. Bro. Wood at church in p. m. Bro. Harding in church. I pray with Gen. Ewell in a. m.

July 27 — Division moves early. Cross mountain at Thornton's Gap. Cool springs all the way up the mountain. Four miles up and four miles down.

July 28 — Rain in p. m. Camp in twelve miles of Madison Court House.

July 30 — Conscripts, thirty-five or forty arrive for our Regiment. Prayer meeting at night.

July 31 — Ride to court house. Much edified by an hour's chat with sister of Rev. Lemon. Begin sermon in p. m. and we suddenly receive marching orders.

Saturday, August 1 — Division moves toward Orange Court House. I go with Bro. Stradley into Gordonville with sick. Moonlight night on the road. Pray with Dr. Adams and his drivers. Get to Regiment one mile beyond Orange Court House before sunrise.

August 2 — Bro. Power preaches in a. m. and I in p. m.

August 4 — Moved camp.

August 6 — Preach in a. m. Prayer meeting at night.

August 8 — Bro. Lacy preaches in Iverson's old Brigade. Prayer meeting in my Regiment at night.

Sunday, August 9 — Bro. Power preaches in a. m., and I preach in p. m., and meet my church members.

August 10 — Sore throat and chest.

August 11 — Meet Chaplains.

August 12 — Go to Richmond.

August 13 — Very busy. Buy good many things for Regiment. Write to Mary.

August 14 — Return to Regiment. Carry fifty Testaments and Psalms, thirteen Bibles, one hundred hymns, etc., to my Regiment and much to others.

August 16 — Bro. Power preaches in a. m., and I in p. m.

August 17 — In camp. Busy every day. Prayer meeting almost every night.

August 18 — Meet Chaplains. Rev. Dr. Broadus preaches. Pleasant meeting. Marry O. L. Pettit to A. H. Layton at Henry Atkins'.

August 19 — Preach in Dole's Brigade.

August 20 — Write to *Advocate*.

August 21 — Fast day. Prayer meeting at sunrise. Preach at 7. Hear Bro. Lacy at Gen. Ewell's at 11. Preach to 2nd Regiment at 4 p. m. Assist in communion in the 14th at night. I baptize two men. Perhaps one hundred and fifty take Lord's Supper.

August 22 — Dine at Bro. Newman's. He and his old Christian wife came to preaching in camp. Her voice, with a thousand male voices, reminded us of the voices of mothers, wives, sisters, and daughters we once heard and now longed to hear again.

Sunday 23 — I preached at 8:30. Bro. Marshall at 11, and I at 4 p. m.

August 24 — Built arbor for meeting.

August 25 — Meet Chaplains at Baptist Church and at court house. Dr. Bocock preaches excellent sermon. Rain.

August 26 — Bro. Lacy preaches in 14th Regiment on "Prodigal Son." Rain.

August 27 — Ride to 2nd Virginia Regiment with Bros. Hopkins and Anderson on question of correspondence with Chaplains elsewhere.

August 28 — Prayer at sunrise. Preach for Bro. Marshall at 8 a. m. Bro, Moore of 12th Alabama Regiment preaches for Bro. Power at 10 a. m.

August 29, 30 and 31. Prayer at sunrise each day and preaching every night. Bro. Howard with me.

Sept. 1 — Meet Chaplains. Dr. Pendleton there. Rev. Dr. Sehon and Rosser come on train. (Rev. Thos. Murphy, of Wilmington, and David Sykes, of Bladen, died Aug. 18.) Two converts during the week. Much interest in 2nd and 3rd. Several penitents and some converts.

Sept. 4 — The Lord's work goes on. Ten quiet, clear conversions at night. Bro. Howard preaches. Ten days furlough comes.

Sept. 5 — Self-denial. Furlough in my pocket; but feel it my duty to remain at my work. Much encouraged by frequent conversions.

(Sixteen years from that day I was to see my wife die in Greensboro. She has been seventeen years in Heaven, as I review my little diary of the trials and toils of war.)

Sept. 6 — Preach for Doles' Brigade. In p. m., Bro Howard, Lawry and I immerse about thirty men. Bro. Powledge, of Georgia, preaches for me at night.

Sept. 7 — Bro. Howard preaches for men at night.

Sept, 8 — Meet Chaplains. Glorious work in the army, thank God!

Sept. 9 — Start home.

Sept. 10 — Get to Raleigh at midnight.

Sept. 11 — Reach home to breakfast.

Sept. 12 — Ride to Orange Church.

Sept. 13 — Preach in M. E. Church in Chapel Hill.

Sept. 16 — Rev. J. W. Jenkins baptizes my fourth son, James Russell.

Sept. 17 — Start to Virginia at 4 p. m. God bless wife and children!

Sept. 19 — Get to Orange Courthouse weak and sick. Walk six or eight miles to Dr. Terryll's.

Sept. 20 — Walk to wagon yard. Ride to Palmyra Church. Preach to Ordinance officers.

Sept. 21 — Get to Regiment near Morton's Ford. Bro. Marshall went with me and preached at Palmyra Church. Sleep in stable at Buckner's.

Sept. 22 — Go in camp near Morton's Ford. Willie's birthday.

Sept. 23 — Preach to Regiment on picket line. Prayers at night.

Sept. 25 — Revs. Rumple and Kilpatrick arrive. Bro. Rumple preaches at night.

Sept. 26 — Bro. Kilpatrick preaches this p. m. Regiments go on picket. Prayer at night.

Sept. 27 — Preach twice on picket. Relieved late. Bro. Rumple preaches at night.

Sept. 28 — Two converts.

Sept. 29 — Write to Prof. Hepburn.

Sept. 30 — Go on picket.

October 1, 1863 — Visit Hoke's Brigade. Bro. Rumple preaches for us.

October 2 — Rain, get wet.

October 3 — Dr. Rosser preaches for us twice.

October 4 — Bro. Kilpatrick preaches a. m. and Bro. Rumple p. m. Fifty or more conscripts arrive for our Regiment.

October 5 — Preach for Battle's Brigade at night.

October 6 — Meet Chaplains at Pisgah Church. Go with Bro. Rumple toward Orange courthouse. Spend night at Mr. Grymes'. Noble family. Man and wife and several daughters seem so glad to entertain us. Some officers there, too. Two armies had been for a long time using the food of that section. We saw no servant in the princely home. The bright young women waited on the table very gracefully. No reference was made to servants or short food supply. The only food we saw or tasted was cornbread, milk and butter. My heart did bless them then, and blesses them now. They accepted the situation gracefully.

October 7 — While we stood by the train at the depot we saw in the ladies' coach a nurse with a little child. I asked her to hold him up that I might see him. I said, "Nurse, please pinch him, I want to hear a baby cry." The ladies looked out to see a crazy man.

October 8 — Corps moving.

October 9 — Leave at 5 a. m. Pass Orange Courthouse.

October 10 — Pass Madison Courthouse.

Experience of a Confederate Chaplain 1861-1865

October 11 — Pass Bethlehem Church. Meet Mrs. Griffin, 86 years old, has never joined any church. Says her husband kept her out 36 years ago. Camp four and a half miles from Courthouse. Rev. Dr. Boyce preaches at night.

October 12 — Pass E. and drive enemy from Jefferson Sulphur Springs.

October 13 — Pass Warrenton. Meet Ed. M. Spillman — a prince.

October 14 — A skirmish early. I remain with wounded at Allison's house.

October 15 — Ten years ago God converted my soul — C. H. Ruffin, of Nash Co., wounded yesterday. Dies in my arms — in perfect peace. Charlie enlisted at 17, and, perhaps, was the wildest boy in his Regiment.

He was very respectful to me, but showed no signs of any care for his soul till April last. About the time I was disappointed in my hopes to go home, he began to seek my company and give good attention to preaching. He became deeply convicted and was happily converted, and I took him into the Missionary Baptist Church, and sent his name to the home church the day I started home. If I had gone home at the time I first proposed, he might not have been converted. Just before he breathed his last I asked him about his case. He sweetly smiled and said: "Bro. Betts as soon as I die I shall go straight to my blessed Jesus!" That was a happy moment to me. As I write about it in October 1896 the joy I feel pays me a thousand times for all the nights I ever slept on frozen ground, snow or mud.

October 16 — Rain a. m. Bury Ruffin. Send sick and wounded to Rappahannock Station by Dr. W. Leave and follow Regiment, and sleep in vacant house at Greenwich. Visit Mr. Green, a British subject. Supper and breakfast with W. T. Hall, of the oldest M. E. Church in Prince William County.

October 17 — Ride on with Bro. Hall. Dine with Mr. Peters. His wife presents me an overcoat and $4.00. Wife's letter tells me that Dr. J. F. Foard sent her a barrel of flour. Camp near W. Junction.

Sunday, Oct. 18 — Pass up R. R. My pony mires and wets my feet. Preach to Dole's Brigade in p. m. Bro. Marshall preaches to my Regiment in p. m. Cross river on Pontoon bridge at night.

Oct. 19 — Brigade crosses in rain.

Oct. 20 — Dine with Rev. Brannin, of Baltimore Conference. Prayer at night.

Oct. 21 — Move camp at night.

Oct. 22 — Fix desk and have fever, as yesterday.

Oct. 23 — Rain. Build chapel. My colonel or other officers commanding my Regiment, always seemed glad to give me any needed help to prepare for preaching — giving me a wagon, a detail of men.

Oct. 24 — Finish chapel.

Oct. 25 — Preach a. m. Prayer meeting p. m. Prayer with Co. "H" at night.

Oct. 26 — Cold. Prayer with Co. "F" at night.

Oct. 27 — Ride to Cook's Brigade. See Revs. Fairly and Plyler. Prayer in Co. "K" at night.

Oct. 28 — Prayer in Co. "E." Write sundry letters.

Oct. 29 — Election for Congress. N. C. soldiers vote. Build my log cabin — 5 feet wide and 6 feet long— nice stick chimney — oil cloth roof. Nice place to read and write and talk to one friend at a time. Sat on my bed (canvas on two poles) and put my feet to the fire, and wrote on a little box desk. Prayer in Co. "C."

Oct. 30 — Finish cabin. Prayer meeting in Regiment.

Oct. 31 — Rain in a. m. Dine with Rev. Brannin. Call on Rev. Wilson, of Chapel Hill, and Rev. Emerson, of Chatham, in Johnson's Brigade. Prayer in Co. "A" at night.

Nov. 1, 1863 — Fine day. Rev. Anderson, Chaplain 4th Regiment, preaches his first sermon at my chapel. Why don't I hear from wife? Thirteen days ago she was not well. May be in heaven! God's will be done! Get letter. All well. Prayer meeting at night.

Nov. 2 — Pastoral work in Regiment. Prayer in Co. "G" at night.

Nov. 3 — Organize Bible class in Co. "G." Dine with Bro. Brannin. Prayer in Co. "B" at night.

Nov. 4 — Pastoral work. Call on Chaplain Murphy of 32nd Regiment. Pray with Co. "G" at night.

Nov. 6— Day with Regiment. Dine with Rev. Dr. Rosser at Bro. Brannin's.

Saturday, Nov. 7 — Hear Dr. Rosser preach to 4th and 14th Regiments. Get bottle of sacramental wine. While reading a letter from wife, a fierce cannonade begins at Kelly's Ford, where the 2nd and 3rd suffer sadly. Lieut. Col. Sillers is mortally wounded. Some are wounded and many captured. Army falls back. I tear down my little house to get my cot out. Had occupied the sweet little home one week. Felt some regret, as I may feel, when called to leave the "earthly house" I now occupy in flesh. Sleep a little on the road, and get to Brandy Station at 2 a. m.

Nov. 8 — Pass on and get to Rapidan Station and spend night. Sorry I could not find Col. Sillers last night. Brigade crosses at Raccoon Ford late at night.

Nov. 9 — Ride down the river to the camp we left a month ago today. Find Brigade there. Snows a little. Prayers at night.

Nov. 10 — Anxious to hear from Col. Sillers, I ride to Orange Court House, but hear on the way he died at Gordonville at 9 a. m. yesterday. Shall I see him on earth no more? Telegraph to learn his body has been sent home, Telegraph to my wife also.

Nov. 11 — Get telegram that Sillers' body is still at Gordonville. Take cars to Gordonsville and find his body nicely packed in charcoal. Return to Orange Court House and spend night at Bro. Walker's, eight miles toward camp.

Nov. 12 — Return to camp. Meet Johnston's division.

Nov. 13 — Just as Bro. McAlpin is about to begin a sermon to us, we get orders to march. We march five or six miles out and go into camp.

Nov. 15 — In camp. Rain in p. m.

Nov. 16 — Rain in a. m. Duel between the armies at Morton's Ford. Division hurries down toward Morton's Ford, but returns to camp. Interesting prayer meeting.

Nov. 17 — Rev. Dr. Bikle prays with us.

Nov. 18 — Ride to Cook's Brigade. See Rev. Plyler, Dodson, Westbrook, etc. Visit Kirkland's Brigade. Sup with old Bro. Newman. Spend night with Bro. Kennedy, 28th N. C. Regiment.

Nov. 19 — Visit Col. Barbour, 37th N. C. Regiment and Col. Barry, 18th, etc. Bro. Kennedy rides with me to Scale's Brigade. Meet Rev. Bennick. Visit Col. Galloway, etc. Return to camp late and weary. I was visiting Colonels to get them to send to our Conference for Chaplains.

Nov. 20 — Preach at night. Disturbed by men in two companies singing near our place of worship; but God was with us and converted L. W. Johnson, Co. A.

Nov. 21 — Rain. Rain. Raise some money to get religious papers.

Nov. 22 — Preach in a. m. Dr. Bikle preaches at noon. Regiment goes on picket at night.

Nov. 23 — Visit Regiment on picket.

Nov. 24 — Ride to Orange Court House. Chaplains do not meet. Rain. Night in Scale's Brigade. Col. Galloway and Col. Coleman give me orders on Bishop Pierce for Chaplains.

Nov. 25 — Go to Richmond.

Nov. 26 — Get to Raleigh at midnight, with Revs. Dodson and Plyler. Night at Bain's Hotel.

Nov. 27 — In city a. m. Buy cloth for grey suit for forty dollars. Visit Legislature. Go to Bio. Alvin's near Cary. Mother just gone to her home in

Harnett. Missed her.

Nov. 28 — Got home to breakfast.

Nov. 29 — Bro. Cunninggim preaches morning and night. I preach in the afternoon.

Dec. 1 — Go to Hillsboro. Call on Aunt Martha Utley. The Lord is with her. Reach Greensboro and stop with Bro. Wm. E. Edwards, near depot.

Dec. 2 — Conference meets in M. E. Church.

Dec. 3 — Army Commission reports.

Dec. 4 — Dr. Deems preaches funeral of Rev. J. C. Brent. Wife comes on night train.

Dec. 5 — Wife and I dine with Sister Bumpass.

Dec. 6 — Bishop Pierce preaches at 11 a. m. Communion at night.

Dec. 7 — Conference closed late at night. Wife and I sup at Mr. Van Bokelin's. Bro. N. F. Reid gives us an order on Bro. Selby for three months' salary.

Dec. 8 — Leave Greensboro at 3 a. m., and go to Hillsboro, and over to Chapel Hill in p. m., with Mrs. John Watson.

Dec. 9 — Pay rent, etc. Gather Bibles, Testaments, etc., for my Regiment.

Dec. 10 — Fast and pray. Preach in M. E. Church.

Dec. 11 — Walk and ride to Mrs. Fearingtons' and get Melvin Baldwin's horse, and ride by William Merritt's and thence to Bro. Purifoy's and then walk home.

Dec. 13 — Hear Bro. William Closs preach at 11 a. m. and Bro. Jenkins at night. Last evening with my family.

Dec. 14 — Leave at 3 a. m. See Bros. Pell and Crowder in Raleigh. Try to see Bro. Hufharn. Leave at midnight.

Dec. 15 — Go to Richmond.

Dec. 16 — Get to Orange Court House. Meet Rev. Mr. Harris, of Lynchburg. Stop at Dr. Black's.

Dec. 17 — Rain and sleet. Cannot get to Regiment.

Dec. 18 — Ride to Regiment near Morton's Ford.

Dec. 22 — Visit Cook's Brigade. See Lieut. Hanner, Revs. Plyler, Dodson, Marsh, and return by 55th Regiment and see Lieut. Hoyle.

Dec. 23 — Snow and very cold.

Dec. 24 — No chimney to my tent. Very cold.

Dec. 26 — Ride to Orange Court House and learn that J. A. Pegram had died suddenly last night at Dr. Black's hospital.

Dec. 27 — Rain. Rain. No preaching. Prayer meeting in Co. E.

Dec. 28 — Get tent of my own. Rain.

Dec. 29 — Clear and very muddy. Meet Chaplains at Pisgah Church. Night in my own tent. Pay fifteen dollars for building wall and chimney.

Dec. 30 — Prayer meeting in some Co. every night — in "G" tonight. Good men. Every night, everywhere, Co. G. has family prayers. Cheatham is sick.

Dec. 31 — Writing and reading until near midnight. Write to Mary. Keep "watch night." On my knees at midnight. A New Year begins! Oh, may it be a good year! May it bring peace to my land! May it carry me and my fellow soldiers to our several homes. Sorry for the follies of the past year. May I be able to spend the new one more for God's glory!

Jan. 1, 1864 — Turns exceedingly cold in p. m. Write for *Recorder* till midnight.

Sunday, Jan. 3 —1 go to Regiment on picket. Prayer in Co. C.

Jan. 4 — Snows all day. In snow getting boards to cover my church.

Jan. 5 — Get three wagons to take my boards to camp. Rev. J. J. Hines, sent by Bishop Pierce to be a Chaplain for Hoke's Brigade, arrives and spends night with me.

Jan. 6 — Carry Bro. Hines to Hoke's Brigade. Make arrangements for his comfort and return.

Jan, 7 — Call to see Bro. Howard, colporter for Johnston's Brigade.

Jan. 8 — Ride to Orange with Bro. Anderson. Ten Chaplains there. No regular meeting. Post office clerks offended. Some time before I had found a large amount of printed matter at the Post Office for my Regiment, which the clerks had neglected to send us from day to day. I wrote a note to the Postmaster and asked him to stir up his clerks. I presume he stirred them up. Borne of the handsome young men were of the right age to be soldiers. They had been detailed as Army postal clerks. My note to the Chief gave them some fear of being sent to ranks. They looked at me in anger and asked me to tell them when I had anything to complain of. I am glad to say I never found occasion to complain again.

Sunday, Jan. 10 — Cold. Prayer meetings in Company quarters.

Jan. 11 — Get a few poles for my chapel.

Jan. 12 — Meet Chaplains at Pisgah. Get poles all cut for chapel.

Jan. 13 — Haul poles and begin my chapel.

Jan. 14 — Still at work on chapel. Chaplains of this division met in my tent yesterday.

Jan. 16 — Get roof and chimneys finished. Having labored with my detail and conducted prayer meeting every night, I feel very much wearied.

Jan. 17 — Preach in chapel a. m. Bible class in p. m. Prayer meeting in Co. I at night.

Jan. 20 — Rev. Henry Hardie calls and prays with me. Bible class at night.

Jan. 21 — Ride by Kirkland's Brigade and see Bros. Webb, Lacy and Smith. Chapel up. Meet Bros. Hines and Paris on their way to North Carolina with Hoke's Brigade. Go late to Lane's Brigade, looking for Bro. Westbrook. Night with Bro. Kennedy.

Jan. 22 — Return to Regiment and find Col. Parker arrived yesterday.

Jan. 23 — Ride with Bro. N. B. Cobb to see Johnston's Brigade and also see Bro. Gwaltney in First North Carolina Regiment. Bro. Robbins, (J. H.) 12th Regiment, arrives and preaches for me.

Jan. 24 — Bro. Harding preaches for me in a.m. Bible class in p. m. Bro. Gwaltney preaches for me at night. Bro. Robbins spends night with me.

Jan. 25 — In camp. Prayer meeting in Co. A. at night.

Jan. 26 — Meet Chaplains at Bro. Booker's chapel in Jones' Brigade. Bro. Cobb preaches. About fifteen Chaplains present. Near twenty chapels being built in this army. Bro. Robbins moves to his Regiment.

Jan. 27 — Exceedingly warm.

Jan. 28 — Bros. Anderson, Robbins and I visit the provost guard and prisoners in Rodes' Division. One prisoner is to be shot.

Jan. 29 — Bro. Robbins and I walk to Bro. Gwaltney's Regiment. I preach.

Jan. 30 — Right unwell. Bro. Robbins spends night with me. Regiment goes on picket.

Sunday, Jan. 31 — Bro. Evans and I visit and preach to provost guard and prisoners. New prison. Visit prisoners also.

Feb. 2, 1864 — Meet Chaplains. Prayer meeting at Bro. Booker's chapel. Write to Henry and his mother. Eight years old today!

Feb. 4 — Walk to Battle's Brigade and see Bros. Currin and Rutledge, Chaplains. Walk to saw mill and thence to 12th North Carolina. Bro. Evans spends night with me.

Feb. 5 — Preach in Bro. Booker's chapel in a. m. Bro. Robbins in Bro. Butler's at night. Bro. Robbins spends night with me.

Feb. 6, 1864 — Revs. F. H. Wood and J. H. Colton arrive. I get a ream of heavy paper. The manufacturers in Wake County sent it to me, at my request, to be given to the men of my Regiment for writing paper. Sheets were very large. Yankees cross Rapidan and our men repel them.

Sunday, Feb. 7 — As my Regiment did not return from picket, I go to see provost guard and prisoners and worship with them. One is to be shot.

Feb. 9 — Meet Chaplains in Presbyterian Church at Orange Court House. Dr. Witherspoon preaches. Gen. Lee is there. Bro. Harding preaches for me at night.

Feb. 10 — I divided a large lot of paper with my men. Bro. Evans, 4th Ga., preaches for me at night.

Feb. 11 — Bro. Gwaltney preaches at night

Feb. 12 — Bro. Jones, 25th Va., preaches.

Feb. 13 — Bro. Nelson, 44th Va., preaches. Dr. Grissom is in camp.

Feb. 14 — Preach to my Regiment.

Feb. 16— Snow on the ground. Bro. Lee, 5th Va., comes to see me and prays with me.

Feb. 17 — Bitter cold.

Feb. 18 — Still bitter cold.

Feb. 19 — At night. Bros. Anderson, Evans, and Power join me and my Regiment in the Lord's Supper.

Feb. 20 — Regiment goes on picket.

Feb. 21 — Preach to 2nd Regiment in a. m., and to 4th at night. Dr. Lloyd spends night with me.

Feb. 22 — Start to North Carolina.

Feb. 23 — Meet Dr. Craven in Raleigh.

Feb. 24 — Get home to breakfast. A. H. Merritt calls and shows us kindness.

Feb. 25 — Ride with family to Merritt's Chapel. Meet Rev. J. B. Martin. Preach for him. Pay two hundred and fifty dollars ($250) for a cow.

Feb. 26-7 — At home.

Feb. 28 — Hear Rev. R. A. Willis preach twice in M. E. Church.

Feb. 29 — Build pen for cow and calf. Bro. Willis sups with us. God keep my family, now and forever.

Mar. 1, '64 — Start at 3 a, m. Meet Bros. Selby, Branson, and Cunninggim in Raleigh. Meet Bros. Burkhead, Henderson, M. C. Thomas, J. B. Williams, and W. B. Richardson on train. Night in Richmond.

Mar. 2 — Meet Bro. H. H. Gibbons.

Mar. 8 — Detained in Richmond by the raiders between us and Lee's army. Bros. Gibbons, Richardson and I visit hospitals and penitentiary.

Mar. 4 — Visit Federal prisoners on Belle Island and hospital No. 24.

Mar. 5 — Bros. Gibbons and Richardson go with me to my Regiment near Orange Court House and spend night with me.

Mar. 6 — Bro. Richardson preaches for me in a. m., and Bro. Gibbons for 2nd Regiment in p. m. Very unwell at night.

Mar. 7 — Walk with Bro. Richardson to his Regiment. Bro. Gibbons preached for me at night.

Mar. 8 — Bro. Richardson preaches for me at night.

Mar. 9 — He leaves for North Carolina against my earnest advice. Bro. Gibbons goes to see R. S. Webb. Squires starts writing school again. I preach at night. My Colonel was kind enough to detail Squires to teach a writing school in my chapel. The Captains allowed men to attend the school when not on duty. (Many men learned to write during the war.)

Mar. 10 — Rain all day. Write many letters. Hear from wife, and Rev. L. S. Burkhead.

Mar. 12 — Walk to see Revs. Colton and Harding. Bro. Gibbons preaches for me at night and spends the night with me.

Mar. 13 — Preach to Daniels' Brigade in church in a. m. and return to Power's Chapel in time for communion, where Bro. Gibbons had just preached. Bible class in my chapel in p. m. I preach at night.

Mar. 14 — Go to Orange Court House with Bro. Gibbons and see him off to North Carolina. Prayer meeting at night.

Mar. 15 — Prayer meeting in K.

Mar. 16 — Prayer meeting in B.

Mar. 17 — Prayer meeting in I.

Mar. 18 — Prayer meeting in F.

Mar. 19 — Regiment goes on picket. I preach for 4th Regiment.

Sunday, Mar. 20 — Hear Bro. B. F, Long preach in 5th North Carolina; communion there. I preach to division provost guard and prisoners in p. m. Bro. Richardson arrives from North Carolina.

Mar. 21 — Visit Daniel's Brigade. Very cold.

Mar. 22 — Meet Chaplains. Dr. Granberry preaches. Gen. Lee there. Snow falls about 18 inches. Bro. Richardson with me.

Mar. 23 — He moves his Regiment.

Mar. 24 — Snow still on ground. My pony gives birth to a female pony.

Mar. 25 — Gov. Vance arrives in Daniel's Brigade.

Mar. 26 — Visit Bro. Richardson. Gov. Vance addresses large crowd.

Sunday, Mar. 27 — Preach in a. m., "Love God." Bible class in p. m. Preach at night, "Love thy neighbor as thyself."

Mar. 28 — Gov. Vance reviews North Carolina troops in this corps and addresses them — "Fellow Tar-Heels!"

Mar. 31 — Finished reading Trumbull's *Christ in History*. Began *Mercy Seat* by Dr. Spring.

Apr. 3, '64 — Preach in a. m. on Psalms I. At night on "Grow in Grace."

Apr. 5 — Snow and rain. Chaplain Westbrook arrives.

Apr. 6 — Go with Westbrook to Lane's Brigade.

Apr. 7 — Preach at night.

Friday, Apr. 8 — Solemn day. Preach twice. Lord, hear and answer the prayers of this day!

Apr, 10 — Preach twice. Rain, rain.

(Note — The kind reader, sitting in a warm room, will please not be offended when I write of "rain." Remember, that a cold rain in April in camp, means something to a soldier.)

Apr. 11 — Rev B. T. Lacy gives his lecture in Rev. W. C. Power's Chapel.

Apr. 17 — Preach to 2nd N. C. Regiment in a. m., and to Division Provost Guard and prisoners in p. m.

Apr. 19 — Meet Chaplains in Orange Court House. Gracious meeting. Rev. Bellinger brings note from Rev. C. W. Westbrook, who is sick. I love Bellinger because he has preached to 18th N. C. Regiment.

Apr. 24 — Preach in a. m. and night. Visit five men condemned to be shot. They are deeply penitent.

Apr. 25 — Preach to prisoners and guard. Pleasant communion service in my chapel at night.

Apr. 26 — Meet Chaplains.

Apr. 27 — Preach in my chapel at night.

Apr. 28 — See three men, from Wilkes County, shot for desertion.

Apr. 30 (Saturday; — Talk with penitents and converts.

May 1 — Hear Brother Power in his chapel, and commune with about one-hundred in a. m. Meet my Bible class in p. m., and preach in my chapel at night. Receive two into the Church.

May 3 — In Richmond. Hear Bro. Christian in Clay Street at night. Good work there.

May 5 — See over a thousand Federal prisoners en route to Orange Court House.

May 6 — Meet many wounded. Pleasant worship with my Regiment. Sizemore of Co. G. killed.

May 7 — Not much fighting. Spend day nursing wounded Federals. Find a son of Rev. B. H. Hedge, of Detroit Conference, M. E. Church, of Co. I. 24th Michigan Regiment. Wounded through left thigh. Did he get home? Is he still living?

May 8 — Marching and fighting. Capt. Mark Moore fearfully wounded. Sergeants Wells, Morrison and Whitehurst killed.

May 9 — Among wounded. Visit Rev, W. B. Owen, Chaplain 17th

Miss. Regiment, who is wounded. Left elbow joint taken out.

May 10 — Terrible fight for Doles' and Daniel's Brigades. Col. Hall of 5th Ala., lost left arm.

May 11 — Visit Capt. S. A. Sutton of 45th N. C. Regiment, who is wounded and was my college classmate. He died there. Lieut. Eubanks, 32nd N. C. Regiment dies in peace.

May 12 — Terrific fighting. Many are wounded and many killed. (Note — Nine years of married life. How many more?)

May 13 — Send off the slightly wounded. My wife's birthday — 27 years! John Hagler dies suddenly.

May 14 — Among the wounded.

Sunday, May 15 — Ride to Brigade and take a shelling. Pray with 2nd and 30th Regiments. Suddenly they are ordered off.

May 16 — Send off a few wounded.

May 17 — Send worst wounded to a new corps hospital. Woniack and Ross die.

May 18 — Send more wounded off to Railroad.

May 19 — Second Corps has a fight. Many are wounded and some killed. Spend part of the day at General Hospital. Am up nearly all night.

May 20 — Very unwell all day. Take medicine.

May 21 — Rev. Evans and I, too unwell to march, report to Dr. Black at corps hospital and receive kind attention.

May 22 — Dr. Black puts me on ambulance. His train moves till in the night.

May 24 — Move on. Get three letters from my wife.

May 26 — Ride through wind and rain to wagon train.

May 27 — Walk past Ashland. Rest and receive kindness from Mrs. Charles Stibbins. Halt at midnight below Hanover Court House.

May 28 — Walk on rapidly and spend some time with my Regiment. Fight begins at twelve.

May 30 — Go to Richmond. Capt. Freeman, Lieut. Lemay and George Stanback are killed.

June 1 — Go to Regiment and find many of my men in Winder Hospital. Busy and very weary. Return and spend an hour with Rev. Dr. Rosser. Spend night at wagons.

June 2 — Meet Revs. Hines, Power, Webb, Plyler and others.

June 4 — At hospital.

June 5 — Preach to my Regiment and hear Patterson and Brown at hospital.

June 6 — Ride into Richmond and hunt up several wounded at sundry hospitals and greatly fatigue myself.

June 7 — Walk, walk, walk. Secure Pell's transfer. Find Burroughs dying. Visit many wounded. Return to wagons.

(Note — Found Wm. E. Pell, son of Rev. W. E. Pell, of N. C. Conference, at Chimborazo Hospital. He told me he wished to get to some other. He was well cared for; but was the only N. C. soldier there and was lonely. I secured his transfer to N. C. Hospital in the same city. He lovingly reminded me of it frequently in Raleigh after the war.)

June 8 — Preach to my Regiment. Messing with Dr. G. L. Kirby.

June 9 — Rev. N. B. Cobb preaches for me. Division moves and he and I go to Richmond at midnight.

June 10 — Visit wounded in two hospitals.

Sunday, June 12 — Rev. Best preaches for me, and Dr. Brown for 4th Regiment.

June 13 — Early's Corps starts to Lynchburg to drive Hunter away. In twenty-nine days we reached Washington City, having passed Lynchburg, the Natural Bridge, Lexington, Staunton, Sharpsburg, Frederick City, etc. What a tramp!

July 9, '64 — Pass J. and rest near Frederick City. Meet Col. Carmack, Mr. Joseph Shawen, Mr. Jones and Mr. Elridge. Receive kindness. Camp near Monocasy. Meet Revs. Kinzie and Reese.

Sunday, July 10 — Move all day and camp near Rockville. Baptize three children for Robert J. Henly, Middle Brook, Md., and one for S. Mullican, Forest Oak, Md. We marched all that Sabbath, but I took time to stop and dedicate those children to the Lord.

July 11 — Pass R. and see Rev. Leach. Move on through excessive heat to the " Blair House," near fortifications around Washington City. First shell from Federal fort falls in a grove near us about 2 p. m.

July 12 — Shelling and sharp shooting. Shearin and Penny killed. Dement mortally wounded. At night we begin to fall back. Tiresome night. Troops halted to rest ten minutes in each hour. Many fell asleep perhaps for eight minutes out of ten. Just before day I was so tired and sleepy that I turned aside to rest. I found a little graveyard near the roadside. I knew some one might steal one of the two horses I had charge of if I tied them and went to sleep. So I laid down and drew the bridle reins through the fence and put my arm into each. I was soon asleep. One horse, I suppose, bit the other. A sudden and fearful pulling of the arm awoke me. Sleep was gone.

July 13 — Pass Rockville and Poolville.

July 14 — Cross Potomac. As I came near the river, a straggling soldier shouted to me and asked me to let him ride the horse I was leading. I told him the horse's back was so sore I could not myself ride him. In a sharp angry tone he replied, "Yes, you think more of a horse than you do of a man." I stopped. As he came near, I said, "Young man, you ought not to speak to me that way. I have waded the James and the Potomac for a sick man to ride my horse. I will now wade this river and let you ride over." He did not wait for me to dismount. He hurried into the warm, shallow water. I trust he and each reader will be slower to judge others than he was that day.

July 15 — Buy a little black mare for fifty dollars from the Quarter Master.

July 16 — Ride early to Leesburg to get shoe and pants mended. Division passes Hamilton and cross mountain at Snicker's Gap.

July 17 — Meet Rev. F. O. Tebbs.

July 18 — Hot fight near Snicker's Ferry. Sergeant Black and others killed. Colonels Wool, Owen, Stallings, etc. Alas!

July 19 — At Hospital. Division moves at night.

July 20 — Division moves by White Post to within one and a half miles of Winchester. Meet Revs. Alliman and Hedges.

July 21 — Move by Middletown and camp on Cedar Creek.

July 22 — Division moves through Strasburg and camps near by.

July 23 — Rest all day and sleep. Hold prayers at night.

July 24 — Whole army moves back to Winchester and drives the enemy with terror from their positions above and about Winchester. Follow them four miles below Winchester and camp. Many wagons burned. Rain at night.

July 26 — Pass on to Martinsburg, but the enemy was gone. Camp near railroad and begin to tear up the track. Hear Bro. Thompson preach.

July 27 — Preach for Doles' Brigade. Bro. Powledge preaches for us.

July 29 — Division moves early to Williamsport Ferry.

July 30 — Move early to the camp we left yesterday. Hear from Mary. Needs bread and money. "Nobody wants to trust you!"

July 31 — Move early to Bunker Hill. Our Regiment sent on picket. Preach to them in p. m.

August 4 — Move through Martinsburg and camp near Falling Water.

August 5 — Move early and cross the Potomac and camp a little beyond St. James College.

August 6 — Move early through rain and stop at Williamsport. Meet Mr. E. P. Steffy and others Quite a stir about those hostages from Hagerstown. Cross river late and camp.

Experience of a Confederate Chaplain 1861–1865

August 7 — Move early past M. and go into old camp near Bunker Hill. Such running and chasing, back and forth, crossing and re-crossing, night and day! Such is war.

August 9 — Dine with Mr. Woolridge.

August 10 — Move early. Go by Mr. Silver's and spend a few hours. Ride to Division four miles north of Winchester.

August 12 — Move and camp two miles N. W. of Strasburg.

August 13 — Troops in line of battle.

Sunday, August 14 — Quiet. Bro. Power preaches in a. m. and I preach in p. m. Prayer meeting at night.

August 16 — Preach to Hoke's Brigade in a. m. and to Johnston's in p. m. Prayer meeting at night.

August 17 — Our men drive the enemy from W. Mills.

August 18 — Pass through Winchester. See mills and wheat barns lately burned by the enemy.

August 19 — Move early towards Bunker Hill. Men go into old camp.

August 20— Sudden alarm. Quiet all the balance of the day.

Sunday, August 21 — Meet Rev. Wm, Hank. Heavy skirmish most of the day, Five in my Regiment killed: Pennington, Williams, Wilkins, Newkirk and Forsythe.

August 22 — Drive enemy through Charlestown and two miles beyond. Heavy rain.

August 23 — Quiet all day. Sup with Bev. J. Wm. Jones and family. Lovely home.

August 24 — Meet Rev. Marsh. Sudden attack on our front. Soon quiet.

August 25 — Corps moves and camps about Shepardstown. Meet Rev. Kilgo and others. My birthday! When shall I spend a birthday with my wife and children?

August 26 — Preach to Regiment. Dine at Mrs. Evans'. Troops all move to Leetown. Meet Chaplain Brooke, of Imboden's Cavalry.

August 27 — Division moves to Bunker Hill.

August 28 — Preach in a. m. Hear from Mary.

August 29 — Men move out and spend day on pike. Spend night in old camp.

August 30 — Brother Rutledge preaches for me Write letter of condolence to Brother L.

August 31 — Division moves to M. and drives out enemy's cavalry. Returns to camp weary. I dine with Harry Thomas.

Sept. 1 — Regiment on picket.

Friday, Sept. 2 — Fast and pray.
Sept. 3 — Day spent in line of battle.
Sept. 4 — Move to Jordan's Springs and spend p. m. in line of battle.
Sept. 5 — Move and drive enemy on Pike and camp near Washington's Farm.
Sept. 6 — Rain, rain.
Sept. 7, 8, 9 — In camp. Meet Rev. Hetrick.
Sept. 10 — Rodes and Ramseur move early to Bunker Hill.
Sept. 11 — Rain. Division moves back and camps midway between Winchester and Bunker Hill.
Sept. 12 — Meet Revs. Heterick, Rogers and Pitzer. Hold prayer meeting.
Sept. 13 — Sup with Mrs. Silver. Meet Chaplain Stringfield and have prayer meeting at night.
Sept. 15 — Regiment on picket.
Sept. 16 — Fast and pray. Hold prayers.
Sunday, Sept. 18 — Preach in a. m.
Sept. 19 — Engage the enemy fiercely near Winchester and drive them, and they drive us. Gen. Rodes killed. Went into private house to see his body after he was brought into Winchester. His wife had spent some time in camp during preceding winter. We fall back to Strasburg, marching all night. Riding alone and very sad, at midnight, I overtake one or two thousand Federal prisoners. They began to sing, " We are going home to die no more." My heart was touched. I shed tears as I thought many of them would die in Southern prisons. Get fifty Testaments, etc. Take position on breastworks near Strasburg.
Sept. 21 — Go to Woodstock to carry Capt. Allen's furlough. He had been wounded and told me he did not wish to be sent to a hospital. I made application for special wounded furlough, that he might go to his parents and sisters in N. C. I took it to the Regimental, Brigade, Division and Corps Commanders and secured each signature and was very glad when I could make him happy by starting him home. This Capt. D. C. Allen was a brave, wicked man; but he lived to be a Christian and his daughter is wife of Rev. E. C. Sell, of the N. C. Conference.
Sept. 22 — Willie's birthday. 7 years. Breakfast with Rev. Armstrong at Woodstock. He after many years gave a bright son to N. C. as a Professor in Trinity College. Return to Regiment. Fight and retreat to Mt. Jackson.
Sept. 23 — Fast and pray. Write to Mary. Occupy Rode's Hill.
Sept. 24 — Retreat slowly under constant cannonading.
Sept. 25 — Pass K. town, Port Republic, and camp near Brown's Gap.

Experience of a Confederate Chaplain 1861–1865

Letter from wife written 16th.

Sept. 27 — Cross above Weir's Cave, driving cavalry, return and camp near Cave. I visit the Cave. Grand sight! Eternal night! Many rooms connected by narrow, crooked, rough passages.

Sept. 28 — Breakfast with Mr. Hansberger. Move slowly towards Waynesborough. Camp at 2:30 a. m.

Sept. 30 — Visit Waynesborough and get wine for Sacrament.

Oct. 1, 1864 — Move through rain and mud and camp three miles beyond New Hope.

Oct. 2 — I preach in a. m. Brother Power preaches at night.

Oct. 5 — Ride to Waynesboro. Spend night at Hospital of 2nd Corps.

Oct. 6 — Go to Richmond.

Oct. 7 — In the City. Very busy.

Oct. 8 — Train late. Spend night at Mr. Goodwin's in Charlottesville.

Sunday, Oct. 9 — Hear Brother Lindsay preach. Attend Sunday School, Get to terminus of Railroad near Staunton. Spend very cold night in the field.

Oct. 10 — Meet Rev. Dice. Start five miles with Capt. Night at Brother Smith's in Mt. Sidney.

Oct. 11 — Get to Harrisonburg. Find Foster and Downes. Start two miles with Dr. Black's train.

Oct. 12 — Get to Mt. Jackson. Find Dr. Triplett's family in great sorrow. Rev. Henry Hardin, of N. C. had married a daughter of Dr. T. and had one child, a son, of one year's age. I had seen the Rev. Mr. Hardin in the Valley a few week's before. I called. Of the woman who opened the door I inquired the whereabouts of Rev. Hardin. She said. "He left here three weeks ago, as your army retreated. We have not heard from him since. He is perhaps in North Carolina. The Federals arrested my aged husband and took him up the Valley that day. They carried him through here yesterday in an ambulance sick. I walked beside him a short distance and handed him some clean clothing. I cannot tell where or how he may be today. Last night my daughter's child died." As she said that she pushed open the door, and I saw a noble looking woman kneeling by the sofa on which lay a beautiful dead child. I knelt down and said, "Let us pray!" The Lord did help us to cast our burden on Him. We prayed for the sick grandfather, for the young father and for the two mothers. I saw no one in the house except the two women and the dead child. When armies were passing through a town every family had to "sorrow alone." As I rose up the young mother remained kneeling, but turning gave me her hand saying: "To whom am I indebted for this great kindness?" I never gave my name with more grateful pleasure. After the war, Rev. Mr. H. was Agent for the American Bible Society and attended sessions of our Methodist Annual Conference. He always said: "Brother Betts, wife sends love to you."

After some years I saw a notice of his death. I felt personally bereaved. Wishing to know the particulars of his death and to offer my sympathies to his family, I wrote to Mrs. H. at J. asking her to tell me about his death and send me his picture. She sent his picture and added that he said he would be on the banks of the River waiting and watching for her. Glory to God for such a hope!

Oct. 13 — My saddle had been stolen during my absence. My baggage had been lost or misplaced. I found mine, Dr. Logan's, Lieut. McNeil's and Mr. Ball's on a forage wagon. Sup with Brother Armstrong in W. and spend the night with our wagons near Fisher's Hill.

Oct. 15 — In line of battle.

Oct. 16 — Quiet in camp. I preach in a. m. and hold prayer meeting at night. Meet Rev. Hines,

Oct. 17 — On picket. Visit Brother Hines.

Oct. 18 — Preach to Johnston's Brigade. Three divisions move all night to get on enemy's flank.

Oct. 19 — Heavy fight and victory in a. m. But our lines are broken in p. m. and we suffer much. Capt. Moore, of Co. F. is killed. Mr. Elliott and Bro. Kittrell, also, are killed. We fall back to Fisher's Hill,

Oct. 20 — Move to camp near New Market.

Oct. 21 and 22 — In camp.

Sunday, Oct. 23 — I preach in camp early and go to hear Chaplain Landstreet of 1st Va. Cavalry preach in M. E. Church of New Market at 11 a. m. In p. m. I preach to Johnston's Brigade.

Oct. 24 — Prayer in camp at night.

Oct. 25 — I preach in M. E. Church at night.

Oct. 26 — Brother L. preaches for our Brigade in a. m. and at M. E. Church at night.

Oct. 27 — Preaching in two churches every night.

Oct. 28 — I fast and pray. Rev. Veitch arrives.

Oct. 29 — Preaching at night.

Sunday, Oct 30 — Love Feast. Preaching and communion. I preach to Johnston's Brigade in p. m. Veitch preaches in church.

Oct. 31 — Chaplains meet in M. E. Church.

Nov. 1, '64 — Solemn day! Set apart in memory of Generals Rodes and Ramseur. I preach in a. m. and Brother Carbon in p. m. Our Brigade

Experience of a Confederate Chaplain 1861–1865

has lost 305 men since we left Winter quarters. They were killed and died of wounds. They left 105 widows and about 300 children.

Nov. 2 — Preaching every night in Lutheran and Methodist Churches. At 11 a. m. a few penitents at prayer meeting.

Nov. 3 — I preach in Lutheran Church at night. Rain.

Nov. 4 — Wind and rain. Regiment goes on picket. I get a furlough of 30 days from 17th instant to visit my family and attend my Annual Conference. I attend preaching in Lutheran Church and sup with Mr. Tidier, a hatter. Mrs. Rutter, Miss Littell and others are kind and attentive.

Nov. 5 — Cold wind. Snows a little. Division moves camp. I visit my Regiment on picket and preach in Lutheran Church at night.

Sunday, Nov. 6 — I preach to Johnston's Brigade. Visit Hines in Hoke's Brigade. Pray with Col. Winston's Brigade. Attend M. E. Church. Rev. Land street preached.

Nov. 7 — Meet Chaplains. Go to new camp.

Nov. 8 — Good meeting at night. Nineteen conscripts come to our Regiment.

Nov. 9 — Prepare seats for our worship.

Nov. 10 — Whole army moves and camps near Woodstock. So we will never use our seats! God grant we may all find seats in heaven.

Nov. 11 — Pass Middletown.

Nov. 12 — Arrange to get Capt. Moore's body up the Valley. Quartermaster gave me a wagon, team and driver. The Colonel of my Regiment detailed a man to assist me. Army was retreating. We pushed on to the grave. It was now dark and snowing. There were two graves! The good man living near by told us one of them was Capt. M's. He knew not which. We dug down till we found a Captain's uniform. We recognized the dead and hastily put body in wagon. A few miles up the pike we got a box I had bought for a coffin. A few miles on we get tan-bark and pack around body. Journey all night. Our army camps at Fisher's Hill. I write to Rev. McGill at Staunton and ask him to look after Capt. M's. body and if he can not send it to N. C. to bury and mark the spot. He did the latter. A few weeks later the body was sent on and rests near old Sparta, Pitt County, N. C.

Sunday, Nov. 13 — Army returns to Edinburg. I rest and dine at Mrs. Hoover's. I surely needed rest after the fatigue and excitement of the last day and night,

Nov. 14 — Return to old camp three miles north of New Market.

Nov. 15 — In camp.

Nov. 10 — Worship with my men. Ride by P's. Division. Dine with

Chaplain Carson at Black's Hospital. Visit Foote and others. Ride late in the night and sleep with Rev. H. M. Brearley who was my classmate many years, graduated with me in 1855 at University of N. C. and is now Chaplain of a S. C. Regiment in Lee's Army.

Nov. 17 — Get to Staunton. See McGill, Downs and others. Go to Waynesboro with Mr. Withrow. All night on the train.

Nov. 18 — Get to Richmond and go on to Danville. All night in darkness.

Nov. 19 — Meet Bill Salmon, of Henry County. He is the only person I ever saw try to kill himself. At Mead's Hotel, Martinsville, Va., in 1856, as my wife and I sat at the table, he sat in front of us and drew his knife across his throat. Some men took him away. Another freight train takes me to Greensboro, N. C. Dine with Rev. Wm. E. Edwards, a brother of Rev. Dr. J. E. Edwards, of Va. Conference. Both were born and raised near G. Spend night with Morris at Durham.

Sunday, Nov. 20 — Get home to breakfast at Chapel Hill, N. C. Rains all day. Nearly nine months since I saw my family. Thank God for his goodness to me and them!

Nov. 21— At home.

Nov. 22 — Visit Mr. Lloyd. Weather turns bitter cold.

Nov. 28 — Visit sundry persons and families.

Nov. 24 — Visit Rev. G. W. Purifey and others. His father, friend of my parents and my boyhood friend, raised three sons, all preachers — Geo. W., James F. and Addison. My oldest daughter was converted under the preaching of Rev. A. F. Purifoy, a son of James F.

Nov. 24 — This day I bought a barrel of home-made syrup and some barrels of corn to feed my family for 1865.

Nov, 25 — At home.

Nov. 26 — Walk several miles visiting Sister Nunn, Cousin Abel Madry and Wm. Strain — good people.

Nov. 27 — Preach in Methodist Church at Chapel Hill, with much comfort.

Nov. 28 — Attend Senior examinations of the University. Take two degrees in Royal Arch Masonry.

Nov. 29 — Meet the bride of Rev. R. A. Willis.

Nov. 30 — Sup with Rev. S. Pool.

Dec. 1 — At home.

Dec. 2 — Sup with Jones Watson, for whom my first son was named, Feb. 2, 1856.

Dec. 3 — Dine with Mrs. White, daughter of Rev. Littlejohn Utley, who knelt by me and told me of Jesus, Oct. 14, 1853, the first and only time I ever presented myself as a peniteut for prayer. Visit University Halls, etc.

Sunday, Dec. 4 — Hear Brother Willis preach twice.

Dec. 5 — Wife and I start to Conference at Mocksville. Reach Salisbury late. Sleep at Mansion House. The preachers go on to M.

Dec. 6 — We ride to Mocksville, in Bro. A. Carter's carriage and stop at W. H. Wyatt's.

Dec. 7 — Conference meets and elects Rev. D. B. Nicholson to preside. In M. we meet Sallie Pailey, who afterward married Rev. S. D. Lee, of the N. C. Conference, whom I loved most tenderly and whose son, Wm. B. Lee, went as a missionary to Brazil. We had many delightful interviews with old friends and new ones during Thursday, Friday and Saturday at Conference.

On Sunday we heard Rev. N. F. Reid preach and enjoyed The Lord's Supper. Dr. McGuire sends us to Dr. Chun's, where we spend the night.

Dec. 12 — We drive to Salisbury and go on to Durham and spend night.

Dec. 13 — Ride early home to Chapel Hill.

Dec. 14 — Very busy at home getting in readiness to leave.

Dec. 15 — Move my family to Stone's house. Get off to Army again. Spend night in Durham.

Dec. 16 — Detained in Greensboro. Visit Sister Bumpass.

Dec. 17 — Visit family of Jones Collier. He sat in church at Chapel Hill, on the night I was a penitent, till all others retired and then gently proposed for me to arise and retire. I long to see him in his heavenly home. Start late and get to Danville and stop at Tunstall House.

Sunday, Dec. 18 — Hear Rev. C. H. Hall preach. Dine and sup with Bro. J. B. Pace, whom I met and loved in Henry County, Va., in 1856. Meet Brother Farley who had an interesting family in Martinsville in 1856. When I asked about his family he told me all were dead. What a change! Then wife and children around his table. Now he eats his food among strangers at the hotel and retires to his lonely room. I leave at midnight.

Dec. 19 — Get to Richmond and spend the night with my wife's father, A. M. Davis.

Dec. 20 — Go to my Regiment near Petersburg.

Dec. 21 — Very rainy.

Dec. 22 — Our Division is ordered off.

Dec. 23 — Capt. Ardry and myself still in camp with the baggage. Both unwell.

Dec. 24 — Division returns late to camp.

Sunday, Dec. 25 — I preach from the song of the angels, " Glory to God, in the highest!" This was the last Christmas of the war. It was Sunday, too.

Dec. 26 — In camp. No mail for three days.

Dec. 29 — Get into my winter quarters — a wall of poles covered with cloth. Chimney of mud and sticks.

Dec. 30 — Visit my brother, Allen Betts, in Co. C. 56th Regiment, just beyond Petersburg, near the enemy. Hear from my wife. Sick. God be with her!

Dec. 31 — Last day of the year. Where shall we be the last day of '65? Some of us were at home with our loved ones, others in Heaven, and others — dreadful thought! A man may fight and die for his country and lose his soul! Mohammed taught that all who died for 'his cause would be saved and some men in this day seem to think that all who are killed in defense of their country are saved; but the Bible assures us "the pure in heart shall "see God."

Jan. 1, 1865 — Snow! Snow! Preach four times in the cabins of my Regiment.

Jan. 2 — Spend day with my brother Allen. Prayer meeting nearly every night. Build stable for pony.

Jan. 17 — Meet Chaplains in Tabb Street Presbyterian Church, Petersburg.

Jan. 18 — Go to Richmond. Spend night with my father-in-law. Meet Mr. Mullins of Henry county, Va.

Jan. 19 — Hear Dr. W. A. Smith on "Oath" in First Baptist Church.

Jan. 20 — Return to Regiment with boxes.

BOXES FOR THE SOLDIERS

Families at home sent thousands of boxes to husbands, fathers, sons and brothers during the war. Some contained pieces of clothing that the soldier would fall and be buried in. We had no chance to wash and dress those who fell in battle. Some of those boxes contained the last food the mother ever cooked for her soldier boy. The soldier seldom could go to the station to claim his box. The Chaplain was often a convenient, cheerful agent. It sometimes involved a great deal of care and fatigue to take boxes from home in N. C. to the army in Va. To hunt them up and get them to the soldiers after they had reached Va. was no light task. But, thank God, "Love lightens labor."

Jan. 21 — Rain and sleet. Brigade goes on picket.

Jan. 22 — In camp. Rain.

Jan. 23 — Hear from wife. In trouble. God help her! Terrible cannonade on our lines till nine at night.

Saturday, ride to McRae's Brigade to see Coin, Jim and A. Davis. Preach on Sunday a. m. and pray with prisoners in p. m.

Feb. 7, 1865 — Rain and sleet. Our Division is ordered off. Three men in my Regiment had to leave their wives in camp. As the troops were ordered to "fall in" I saw the situation and made haste to tell the brave men that I would take their wives to the depot and see them start for their homes in N. C. The men may have lived to go to their homes I wish I knew. That was a touching scene. The wife thought she might never see her husband again. She heard the men were in camp around Richmond. She got Grandma or someone to take care of the other children while she took the babe to see its father in camp. They reached the camp. Both were so happy for two or three days. Now! That drum calls the man to give his babe a hasty kiss (it may be the last one) and turn away from his wife, and go out to fight and face death. I secured an ambulance and took the three good women to the depot. I wish I now had their names.

Feb. 8 — "Peace Commission" fails.

Feb. 9 — Regiment get away.

Feb. 10 — Fast and pray.

Feb. 11 — After prayer meeting in Co. B, I am taken suddenly and seriously ill and stay in bed three days and nights.

Feb. 14 — Revs. Ira T. Wyche and T. A. Cunninggim arrive in our Brigade. Bro, W. stops with me; Bro. C. with Rev. B. F. Lacy. Each preaches at night.

Feb. 20 — Brigade goes on picket.

Feb. 21 — Division moves to Sullivan's depot. I attend Chaplain's meeting.

Feb. 25 — Brigade returns to camp. I carry John (Capt. Allen's negro servant) to hospital with typhoid fever.

Feb. 26 (Sunday) — I preach.

Feb. 27 — Visit my brother, Allen Betts.

March 3, 1865 — Regiment goes on picket. Revs. O. J. Brent and W. H. Moore arrive from N. C. and stop with me.

March 4 — Brother Brent goes to Richmond. Brother Moore remains with me.

March 5 (Sunday) — I walk nine miles and preach to my Regiment in picket camp.

March 10 (Friday) — I fast and pray. Preach to my Regiment six times in their quarters. Rain all day. God help our nation in this sore extremity!

March 12 (Sunday) — Preach to my Regiment. Hold prayers at night.

March 13 — Brother Power preaches at night.

March 14 — Hear from wife and Brother Willson. Preach at night. Brother Power and I alternate in our chapel, preaching every day and night.

March 18 — Go to Petersburg to see John (negro servant) nearly dead. Get him into hospital.

March 19 (Sunday) — Preach to Weiseger's Brigade in a. m. and ours in p. m.

March 20 — Brigade moves near Dunlap's and relieves Thomas' Ga. Brigade.

March 21 — Meet Chaplains in Petersburg, and see John and Capt. Allen.

March 22 — Go by 11th N. C. Regiment and spend night in 56th with my brother. Preach to R.'s Brigade.

March 24 — Meet Cousin Grey Utley in P. He raised three daughters. Two became wives of Rev. L. S. Burkhead, D. D. One Sunday night in October, 1853, Rev. J. L. F. opened the doors of his church in Chapel Hill to receive members. Just as I started forward, that good man, Grey Utley, began to sing "Jesus, I my cross have taken." That soft, sweet voice and the sentiment of that hymn stir my heart tonight in October, 1897, as I write these lines — 44 years after that solemn scene. Jim Davis, of Chapel Hill, my wife's cousin, comes to see me.

March 25 — Brigade moves and I start home on "leave." It was my last furlough, though I had no idea that I was to see the soldiers and Chaplains no more. How tender would have been the leave-taking, if I had known it was my last sight of those with whom I had been so long associated.

March 26 (Sunday) — Heard Rev. Christian preach at Clay Street in Richmond in a. m., and start to N. C. at 6 p. m. It was the last sermon I was to hear in Va. during the war. All night on the railroad.

March 27 — Get to Durham and spend night.

March 28 — Reach home and find all well. How happy to be with my wife and little ones. My oldest son had but lately given his heart to God and joined the Church.

March 31 — Ride thirty miles horseback and spend night with my brother, A. N. Betts.

April 1, '65 — Walk five miles to see my mother in the home of Allen

Betts. Visited sister Jane Betts, widow of my brother, Andrew, who was captured as captain of his company on R. Island in 1862, and reached home on parole to die. He took his eldest son with him. He died in prison. Spent night with C. H. Cofield, who was my guardian for ten years of my boyhood.

April 2 (Sunday) — Preach at Myatt's schoolhouse. Spend night with my youngest brother, Archibald. "When shall I see my mother again?" Those words were written with the expectation of returning to Lee's Army in a short time.

April 3 — Return to Chapel Hill with sick horse. Spent week at home gardening. Receive bacon and lard I had bought on the Harnett line, thirty miles away. Hurrying up to be ready to return to the Army.

April 9 (Sunday) — Heard Brother Willson preach. During this week heard that Lee had surrendered! Sad news. Johnston's Army passed through Chapel Hill. We knew Sherman would soon be in. I did not wish to meet him. I told some of my friends I was going with Gen. Johnston's Army. Rev. Dr. Charles Phillips tenderly told me to go on and my friends would take care of my family. After midnight I kissed my wife and children and mounted a mule and rode away, thinking I might not see them in months or years. I rode all night, crossing Haw River, overtook Johnston's Army, and reported to Brig. Gen. Hoke, who assigned me to duty as Chaplain to 17th N. C. Regt. We camped a few miles from Greensboro for two or three days till we heard we were to be surrendered. I rode to Greensboro one day and met Rev. Dr. John B. McFerrin of Nashville, Tenn., at the home of good Mrs. F. M. Bumpass. The night following the tidings of our contemplated surrender was a still, sad night in our camp. Rev. W. C. Willson, the Chapel Hill pastor, was with us. We had preached a few times in that camp; but that night we made no effort to get the men together. In little, sad groups they softly talked of the past, the present and the future. Old men were there, who would have cheerfully gone on, enduring the hardship of war, and protracted absence from their families, for the freedom of their country. Middle aged men were there, who had been away from wives and children for years, had gone through many battles, had lost much on their farms or stores or factories or professional business; but would that night have been glad to shoulder the gun and march forward for the defense of their "native land." Young men and boys were there, who loved their country and were unspeakably sad at the thought of the failure to secure Southern Independence.

Rev. W. C. Willson and I walked out of the camp and talked and wept together. As I started back to my tent — to my mule and saddle, I should say, for I had no tent — I passed three lads sitting close together, talking softly and sadly. I paused and listened. One said, ' ' It makes me very sad to think of our surrendering." Another said, "It hurts me worse than the thought of battle ever did." The third raised his arm, clenched his fist and seemed to grate his teeth as he said, "I would rather know we had to go into battle tomorrow morning." There was patriotism! There may have been in that camp that night generals, colonels and other officers who had been moved by a desire for worldly honor. Owners of slaves and of lands may have hoped for financial benefit from Confederate success. *But these boys felt they had a country that ought to be free!* I wish I had taken their names. And I wonder if they still live. They are good citizens, I am sure.

Next day I mounted my mule and started to Chapel Hill, intending to surrender there. I took along a negro servant and horse for a friend. At sunset we met an old man at his spring near his house. I politely asked to be permitted to spend the night on his land. He objected. I said, "Boy, take off our saddles and halter our horses." The farmer quickly said, " If you will stay, come up to the house." I slept on his porch.

MY FIRST INTERVIEW WITH A FEDERAL SOLDIER ON DUTY

I had seen many of them dead, wounded, or prisoners. Near Chapel Hill one rode up to my side. The Blue Coat and the Grey chatted softly and sparingly. He kindly offered to show me the way to headquarters. I thanked him and told him I would ride to my house and see my family and report myself later. The town was full of Federals. Each home had a guard detailed by the commanding General. My guard was a faithful, modest fellow. In due time I called at headquarters and was paroled.

APOLOGIA

The Reverend A. D. Betts, D. D., author of the foregoing diary, is my own honored and beloved father; and, although he has, neither suggested nor advised my action herein, I have taken the liberty to append some estimates of his worth and work, which will be appreciated by others who have known and loved him and received spiritual benefit from his Christly ministry.

The word of affectionate appreciation ought often to be offered our deserving fellow travelers along life's journey. Better this, by far, than reserving fulsome eulogy for the completion of their moral task. Uttered now, it will gratify and most likely cheer the weary pilgrim. Fear thou not it may foster inordinately vanity, for hardship enough has befallen to forefend such folly. Most of all will it please the Master if the loving meed of one's worth be accorded duly and sincerely.

W. A. BETTS.
South Carolina Conference.

WAS with "Uncle Betts" nearly five weeks, three years ago, and no man ever impressed me more, as being Christ-like — living holiness.

His success, as the world counts success, has not been very great, yet thousands whom he has led to Christ, call him blessed, and will be a crown of rejoicing in the better world.

— *Rev. J. V. Williams, L. P., in N. C. Conference.*

CALLED forth by a few well-chosen words by the Editor, several brethren have published in the *Raleigh Advocate* their appreciation of Rev. Dr. A. D. Betts, the oldest effective member of the Conference.

The close of the article of Rev. John N, Cole fitly describes the man: "A man without an enemy — a man that never lost a friend — a man beloved by everybody, and that himself loves everybody, and that loves God best, is the venerable Dr. Betts." The writer once heard a prominent Episcopalian vestryman say that he would give any three clergymen of his acquaintance for Dr. Betts and throw in a Bishop extra.

— *Correspondent Nashville Christian Advocate, March 10, 1904.*

IF there is anywhere a rich mine, it is the character of Dr. A. D. Betts. I have known him for more than fifteen years, and the more I know him the more strongly am I convinced of his simple greatness — "simple," because his is the meekness which is destined to become the inheritor of the earth; "greatness," because his whole life is based upon goodness. It is refreshing to be in his presence. He always carries sunshine with him. No other man in North Carolina Methodism will leave to the generations a richer bequest than will be left by Dr. Betts.
— T. N. Ivey, D. D., Editor Raleigh Christian Advocate.

THE Rev. A. D, Betts, D. D., has nearly rounded out a half-century of faithful and successful work in the Methodist itinerancy. He is still vigorous and gives promise of several years of active service. He is furnishing a beautiful lesson of how to grow old gracefully. He is a man of the highest character and has the full confidence of all the people. He is a man of great faith and zeal and energy. He has prayed in more homes, probably, than any other man in North Carolina. He regards any place where souls can be won for Christ a good one, and has gone cheerfully to every appointment assigned him. He is greatly beloved by his brethren.
— F. D. Swindell, D. D., of the N. C. Conference.

I WANT to say in reference to "Uncle Betts," that he was once my pastor, and the bonds of love then sealed still remain. He has never forgotten the covenant then entered into with my people.

He is emphatically a seed-sower, and though results may not always appear, eternity will reveal the good he has done. I have seen him under different circumstances, even surrounded by sin — and why should not a preacher go where sin is? — Yet he never forgot his Master's business. He does a great deal of personal work, and it would be well to remember, that however indifferent one may appear, often beneath there is a soul hungry for some word of encouragement.
— M. Mial, Esq., Lay Member of N. C. Conference.

MY first intimate acquaintance with this devout man of God was when we roomed together at the Annual Conference in Greensboro, N. C. in 1889. I was being received on trial. He began then to show a fatherly interest in me, and has never ceased to do so. With Dr. Betts

religion is a most vital, practical experience, and that, too, " every day and every hour." His life is marked by regular and constant devotion to God and duty — cheerful submission to church authority and willing service in any portion of the Lord's vineyard — diligent pastoral ministration and personal watchfulness for souls. No man among us more completely has the confidence and love of both preachers and laymen; for, like Caleb, "He wholly follows the Lord God of Israel."
— *Rev. R. H. Broom, of the North Carolina Conference.*

It was early in the seventies (1874 I think) when my pastor, Rev. A. D. Betts, came to the door of our humble little home, and on being invited in, said: "No, I have just called to take your subscription to the *Advocate*. You can hand me $2.00 any time, if not convenient to pay now." "Goodbye, Bro. Hoyle; good-bye, Sister Hoyle, God bless you." It is a model plan for pastors to get their flock to read the church paper. Before that morning I had never been a subscriber to my church paper, and I don't think I had ever been asked to subscribe. Since that time the *Advocate* has made its weekly visits to our home, except for a few months in 1878 or 1879. I thank Bro. Betts that he did not give me the chance to tell him that "money was scarce," or that "I was taking as many papers as I could read." O how much I would enjoy seeing Bro. Betts again. Our first pastor in our married life, and the one who baptized our first-born. Betts, Bobbitt, Black and Blair — have given much strength and added many years to the life of the *Advocate*.
— *P. A. Hoyle, Esq., Newton, N. C. in North Carolina Christian Advocate*

A MAN by nature richly endowed — a fragrant and generous soul to whom goodness is easy and natural under the sunshine of grace. He does not have to study to be good; goodness is not a thing that he has to purpose in his soul — it is the opening of his soul in its purely natural life under grace — just as beauty and fragrance are the opening of a flower in its own sweet life.

Doctor Betts is the born gentleman, full of all human excellencies, unselfish, large-hearted and noble, ready for every good word and work. He has lived to make the world brighter and purer and sweeter. He is a lifter of burdens from the hearts of his fellowmen. His pathway is a pathway of light. He is the child of the day. Goodwill to all men has been the song of his life.

The love of Christ has been the sweet constraint of his labors. And in it all he has had the peace of God in his heart and has been one of the happiest of the servants of the King.

A man without an enemy — a man who never lost a friend — a man beloved by everybody and that himself loves everybody and that loves God best, is the venerable Doctor Betts.

— *Rev. J. N. Cole, D. D., of the N. C. Conference.*

SINCE about 1859 we have well known Rev. A. D. Betts, D. D. He is an alumnus of the University of North Carolina, and one of the most consistent Christians and profoundly religious men we have had the pleasure of knowing. He is without guile, or hypocrisy, or evil speech. He was one of the best and most devoted chaplains in the Confederate service.

General Lee was so greatly impressed with the devotion, fidelity and purity of this good man that he spoke of him as "that model chaplain." He is one of the most consistently devout, consecrated, and useful ministers we have found in a long life. We hold him in high esteem and have known no Methodist preacher of more exalted qualities, of a higher sense of responsibility to God, or of more devotion to his work as an ambassador for Christ. We consider it alike a pleasure and honor to have had such unbroken and fruitful association and friendship with him. We hope his years may yet be many in this land he loves, and has so obediently and faithfully served, and that he will enter into his final rest with an assured confidence in his salvation through an abiding faith in the blessed Son of God.

— *T. B. Kingsbury, LL. D., of Wilmington, N. C.*

IT has been my good fortune to know, esteem and love "Brother Betts" for more than forty years, and my life has been made better for having enjoyed so rich a bounty. I flatter myself to hope that my life bears the water-marks of some, at least, of the many good qualities of this faithful man of God, who is humble, lovable and consecrated. His consecrated life, filled with love for his fellow-man, and abounding in good works, like the "alabaster box," yields a most delightful perfume.

I well remember the day of his graduation, and can recall with distinctness the subject of his graduating thesis. It was fine and made a most marked impression. I am proud that all these forty odd years, I have been blessed with, his friendship. May his evening tide be as sweet and mellow as the "sunset's radiant glow," and may he be spared yet many years to tab-

ernacle in the flesh, that his life and example may abide as a benediction with all " who love his appearing," and when he crosses the bar, "may he meet his pilot face to face."
I am glad of an opportunity to add my tribute to one so worthy.
— *Gen. Julian S. Carr, Durham, N. C.*

I HAVE known Rev. Alexander Davis Betts, often in North Carolina affectionately called Father Betts, for over fifty years — as a student of this University, as a citizen and as a minister. I lived for twenty years in the county of his birth, in which he dwelt up to manhood. For years he was a Trustee of this institution, when I was its President. I therefore write of his character of my own knowledge.

He is of excellent stock and has inherited the virtues of his forbears. Always he has been conspicuous for sincerity and truthfulness, for courage to do right, for faithfulness to every duty, for undoubting faith in the God of the Bible. He has striven to follow in the steps of our Holy Savior. His studies have never resulted in disturbance of his creed by the speculations of the, so called, Higher Critics, He has been a loyal, well disciplined, undaunted soldier of Christ and has never lost any part of his panoply. Duty has always been his guiding star. He has not swerved from the path to it to the right or the left. His heart is tender as a woman's for the relief of distress and bold as a lion's in conflict with error. Take him all in all he possesses in full measure all the Christian graces.
— *Kemp P. Battle, LL. D., Prof. Univ. of N. C.*

MY recollections of Rev. A. D. Betts, D. D., when I was his Presiding Elder, causes me to estimate him as, perhaps, the most unselfish man amongst us, regarding his fields of labor. Once at Conference, when it was understood between us that he would move, he waited until the appointments had been read, and final adjournment had been had, to deliver his wife's message of love to me, and yet kindly suggested that I could not have been consciously influenced in the making of his appointment by knowledge of such affectionate esteem. On another occasion when developments after an early fourth Quarterly Conference impressed him that some of the brethren would prefer a change in preachers at Conference, he by letter asked me to authorize him to make appointments for me to preach at some of his churches in the week, his Circuit being located between the Circuits I had published quarterly meetings for including the

Experience of a Confederate Chaplain 1861–1865

Sabbaths preceding and succeeding the week named, and thus he brought me again to his Circuit that the brethren should have an opportunity to talk with me, and that I should have opportunity to further study the needs of the work, and he himself magnanimously and cheerfully consented that the change be made, and as to where he should be sent I could only learn from him that he was ready to go anywhere. Indeed, I found him always the very embodiment of the spirit of our itinerancy.

Another recollection of Dr. Betts: It was at Trinity College at a commencement. I had gone to his room, and my son coming for me I arose to go, when the Doctor laid his hand on me and asked me to wait and have a word of prayer with him, and closing the door we three knelt together and it was not difficult to lead in that prayer; for I was in the prophet's chamber. I love this man of God.

— *Rev. J. T. Gibbs, of the N. C. Conference.*

REV. A. D. BETTS and I were college mates at the University of North Carolina, he being of the Class of 1855 and I of the one just preceding. We were also members of the Dialectic Society, a literary society of great value to the institution in those days when membership of that or the Philanthropic, the other meritorious literary society was compulsory. For some time after the resuscitation of the University in 1875 he was a member of the Board of Trustees of his Alma Mater, and I was associated with him in that capacity. Before and since I have had the pleasure of meeting him occasionally. Mr. Betts having been raised on a farm, with inadequate school advantages in his neighborhood, was older than the average college student when at Chapel Hill, and his influence on his fellows was correspondingly greater. He was faithful to every duty and graduated with honor. He was then a member of the Methodist Church and had the moral courage and independence to avow and live up to his principles, even in company with young men who "cared for none of those things." in manner and disposition he was ever cheerful and cordial, and from observation I would say that cheerfulness has always been one of his leading characteristics. Is it not due to this as much as to his habits of temperance in meat and drink, that he is still hale and hearty after passing the Psalmist's limit of threescore and ten? His cheerfulness has made others happier, while it has made him less careful as to the ills that attend advanced years. Not being a member of the same Church as Mr. Betts, I cannot speak of him as a preacher, from personal knowledge; but from the fervency of his prayers on public occasions at the University and elsewhere and his manner as a speaker in meetings of the Board of Trustees, I doubt not he is an earnest and successful preacher of the Gospel, and as a pastor his ministrations could not but be acceptable to the many flocks of which he has charge as a member of the Methodist Conference. May he be spared to his Church and State many years longer!

— Hon. R. H. Battle, Raleigh, N. C.

I FIRST saw Rev. A. D. Betts, D. D., at a Monday night prayer meeting in the Seaman's Bethel, in Wilmington, N. C. in 1866. He made an impression upon my mind that night as a very earnest, zealous, godly man, full of the gladness of religion. I then thought that he was acquainted with his Lord and was in great peace. In 1876, I was received on trial into the North Carolina Conference. Since that time we have had the annual greeting without a break that I remember. We were pastors in the same town. It was a real pleasure and much profit to be associated with him in the same pastorate. I received much benefit from the association. While on the Washington District as Presiding Elder, we were together again, where I saw Doctor Betts from another standpoint. First, in my youth, I saw him in the prayer meeting.

Next, as a brother preacher in our Conference. Again, as pastors in the same charge, and subsequently associated as Presiding Elder and pastor. He has always been the same earnest, sweet spirited representative of his Lord. I always loved to attend his Quarterly Meetings, His life, his work, was a benediction to me and I left his circuit better for the association. I looked at him during our last Conference at Goldsboro and thought surely no man has ever passed so many years with so little change. Remarkably little difference in physical appearance. Just as full of energy, just as earnest, just as anxious for conversions as back in the sixties.

He has always tried to sow seed in the by-ways. His horse soon learned to stop on meeting any one. Only a minute to ask about the spiritual condition and he was gone, singing as he went. Was that time wasted? I heard a preacher say at the District Conference in LaGrange, that the brief question, "Are you on the road for the Better Land?" by Doctor Betts, fastened conviction upon him and led him in contrition to his Lord. I always appreciated his prayers for me, and regarded his visits to our home as a benediction. Here and there in my journeys I found old veterans who have very warm commendations of Doctor Betts as a faithful, conscientious chaplain during the Confederate war. He yet holds a very large place in the hearts of the old soldiers. Yes, he is now on the downward slope in

life's journey. The material sun is getting lower, but in the spiritual life his sun is yet at meridian and will not go down, but grow brighter and brighter until the perfect day. God forever bless him and all of his.
— Rev. F. A. Bishop of the N. C. Conference.

MY personal acquaintance and association with Rev. A. D. Betts, D. D., began twenty years ago, and has continued with an intimacy akin to family ties. For a number of years we came in contact almost daily. Twenty years! Quite a span in life, and much may be accomplished; but when embraced between the fifty-second and seventy-second years, not much that is of interest to the public. That is a period when men begin to plan for retirement, superannuation, etc. The history making epoch is past. Bodily infirmities, in the case of the veterans of the Confederate war at least, from exposure and hardships of various kinds claim the attention. Instead of benefactors to the human race, they become themselves beneficiaries of a willing and generous constituency. Our hero stands out a notable exception to the rule. There is nothing in common with this class except the mere fact of age. He possesses a perfectly sound, though somewhat frail body, and a mind as active as in youth — a result largely due to his strict observance of the laws of health, and wonderful self-control: To properly appreciate the character of this great and good man, certain facts must be borne in mind. One of the best educated men of the day, with high social and family connections, with ability to fill with ease and honor any position in the gift of the people — to deliberately turn his back upon all such opportunities, and voluntarily take upon himself a work comparatively menial, a work fraught with danger to himself, as well as hardship, and the remuneration a mere pittance — is this not most remarkable in an age of self-aggrandizement and commercialism? A complete crucifixion this, of self for others, and withal a cheerful and happy disposition, almost angelic. He is a practical Christian, practicing six days what he preaches on the Sabbath. Contact with such a man is a benediction. As a preacher and pastor and citizen, in all he is a model. But it is in the sick room, especially among the poor, that he shines with peculiar splendor. This is the work he selects, and is never so happy as when engaged therein. He does not wait to be sent for, nor even for such cases to be reported to him. He is always on the alert, and where needed most there he is to be found. Not only does he share his money, but where that is not sufficient to relieve all the needs, he supplies the deficiency with personal service. How often has he been seen with arms full of wood from a neighboring saw-mill, buckets of water, etc., hastening to relieve suffering! This of course is outside of his ministration to their spiritual needs.

Young men have a special interest for Dr. Betts. In his lodge (Odd Fellows), on the streets, everywhere, he is their friend. The desire to help others seems to overshadow all other considerations. His favorite song, as I have so often heard him in his room at my home, before joining the family at the breakfast table, is, "Help us to help each other, Lord." This correctly illustrates the principle of his life. Donations to him, whether money or otherwise, are used to help others. He never heralds his work to the world, for truly his left hand is ignorant of what his right hand does. Of all my acquaintances, he is the best and greatest — not as the world calls great, perhaps, for he is to be measured by no such standard.

The influence for good of the very presence of this godly man in a community cannot be estimated in words, for it is greater far than volumes of sermons and discourses. May he be spared many years of health and usefulness, is the prayer of one who loves him next to his own immediate family!

— N. H. Street, M. D., of New Bern, N. C.

BIOGRAPHICAL

Alexander D. Betts, son of Wm. and Tempe Utley Betts, was born in Cumberland (now Harnett) county, N. C. August 25, 1832. Brought up on a farm till seventeen years of age when just for fun he mounted a wild, young steer which threw him, so badly crippling him that he could not do farm work. That accident put him in a classical school at Summerville, whence he went to the University of North Carolina. He was converted there October 15, 1853, cinder the ministry of Rev. J. L. Fisher of the Methodist Episcopal Church, South, and joined that church a few days thereafter. He attended the North Carolina Conference at Raleigh the following month, and has been permitted to attend fifty others without missing one. He soon felt that God called him to preach the gospel, and received license while yet a student. He was graduated June 7th, 1855, having married Miss Mary E. Davis of Chapel Hill, May 12th. He taught school five months at Pittsboro the next fall. Just after Conference, 1855, Bishop Andrew sent him as supply to Henry Circuit, Va. His first Presiding Elder, Rev. John Tillett, was a great blessing to him, writing to him between quarterly meetings and encouraging him in many ways. He joined the North Carolina Conference at Greensboro in 1856, and served charges in Cumberland, Sampson, Brunswick and Bladen before the war. While preaching at Smithville (now Southport) Gov. Clark, at the request of the officers of the 30th North Carolina Regiment, sent him a commission as their Chaplain, October 25th, 1861.

After the war he served charges at New Hanover, Granville, Wake, Anson, Cabarrus, Guilford, Duplin, Carteret, Jones, Nash, Hyde, Wilson, Chatham, Robeson, Richmond, Craven, Pitt, Cumberland and Harnett.

The mother of all his children died in Greensboro, September 5, 1879. She had kept up family worship every day in her husband's absence. October 26, 1881, God gave him Priscilla M. Debnam of Wake County, N. C. to help him and his motherless children to get to Heaven.

Eighth Annual Meeting and Reunion of the United Confederate Veterans

THIRD DAY'S PROCEEDINGS
Friday, July 22, 1898

When General Gordon called the Convention to order at 10:10 yesterday morning, there were fully 15,000 people in the hall. It was impossible to find seats, and the aisles were packed and jammed with Veterans struggling to get close to the platform.

"It was the habit of our great chieftain, Robert E. Lee," said General Gordon, "after the most brilliant victories ever won by the Confederate armies, to ascribe his success to the providence of God. When I stood yesterday listening to the songs of praise to that God to whom Lee looked for help and support, it carried me back, as it did you, to those good old scenes in the midst of strife, when the soldiers used to sing praises to Almighty God; and I want you, as becomes us dependent on His will, to again unite in singing that grand old hymn, *Praise God, from Whom All Blessings Flow*.

That vast audience stood and sang that old song as probably they had never sung it before. The melody from 10,000 throats wafted out from that big building toward heaven, and the angels themselves must have joined in the refrain.

Rev. Dr. Betts, of North Carolina, then led in prayer as follows:

"Oh, God, our Heavenly Father, we do thank Thee that Thou dost allow us to call Thee Father. Have mercy upon us today and forgive all our shortcomings. We thank Thee for Thy great goodness to us — for watching over these old warriors so long with such tender mercies. God bless every one of them; they deserve Thy blessing. We do thank Thee that Thou hast spared them to come through the perils of war to be here today. God bless our commander-in-chief. May he be strong in the faith of the Dying Savior, and may he gather with us on many more such occasions as this before the end of his earthly existence. Bless every home represented in this great gathering. Bless Atlanta and all Atlanteans. Remember, God, every home in this great city. Be with this great nation in the war it is now waging against Spain, and remember the prayers of many tender-hearted mothers on both sides of the great Atlantic. Be with us in our deliberations, and stir the hearts of those who have not yet accepted the religion of the Lord Jesus Christ. Amen."

Dr. Betts was so filled with the inspiration of the scene that he embraced General Gordon, saying: "God bless you my noble old Commander, I hope and believe we will meet on the other shore," and asked the audience to sing that old familiar hymn, *Brother, Will You Meet Me*. He started the air himself, and nearly everybody in the house joined in the singing:

> "Say, brother will you meet me,
> Say, brother, will you meet me,
> Say, brother, will you meet me,
> On Canaan's happy shore?"

> "By the grace of God we'll meet you
> On Canaan's happy shore.
> There we'll shout and give Him glory,
> On Canaan's happy shore."

THE NINTH OF APRIL, 1865

(From the *London Spectator*)

It is a Nation's death-cry! Yes, the agony is past;
The stoutest race that ever fought, today hath fought its last.
Aye, start and shudder, well thou mayst! Well veil thy weeping eyes!
England, may God forgive thy past; man cannot but despise.

Yes, shudder at that cry that speaks the South's supreme despair;
Thou that could'st save and saved'st not, that could'st and did'st not dare,
Thou that had'st might to aid the right and heart to brook the wrong;

Weak words of comfort for the weak, strong hands to help the strong.
That land, the garden of thy wealth, one haggard waste appears!
The ashes of her sunny homes are slaked with patient tears —
Tears for the slain who died in vain for freedom on the field —
Tears, tears of bitterer anguish still for those that lived to yield.

The cannon of his country pealed Stewart's funeral knell;
Her soldiers' cheers rang in his ears when Stonewall Jackson fell;
Onward o'er gallant Ashby's grave swept war's triumphant tide,
And Southern hopes were living yet when Polk and Morgan died.

But he, the leader on whose word those captains loved to wait,
The noblest, bravest, best of all, hath found a harder fate.
Unscathed by shot and steel, he passed through many a desperate field;
Alas! that he lived so long, and only lived — to yield!

Along the war-worn, wasted ranks that loved him to the last,
With saddened face and weary pace the vanquished chieftain passed.
Their own hard lot the men forgot, they felt what his must be;
What thoughts in that dark hour must wring the heart of General Lee.

The manly cheeks with tears were wet, the stately head was bowed,
As breaking from their shattered ranks around his steed they crowd.
"I did my best for you!" 'Twas all those quivering lips could say;
Ah, happy those whom death had spared the anguish of that day.

* * * * * * * * *

Sunny South, weep on! Weep the lives given to thy cause in vain;
The sons who live to wear once more the Union's galling chain;
The homes whose light is quenched for aye; the graves without a stone;
The folded flag, the broken sword, the hope forever flown.

Yet raise thy head, fair land! Thy dead died bravely for the right;
The folded flag is stainless still, the broken sword is bright.
No blot on thy record is found, no treason soils thy fame;
Weep thou thy dead; with covered head we mourn our England's shame!
— *W. R. Greg.*

THE BIVOUAC OF THE DEAD
By Captain Theodore O'Hara

The muffled drum's sad roll has beat,
The soldier's last tattoo;
No more on life's parade shall meet
That brave and fallen few.
On Fame's eternal camping ground
Their silent tents are spread,
And glory guards with solemn round,
The bivouac of the dead.

No rumor of the foe's advance
Now weeps upon the wind,
No troubled thought at midnight haunts;
Of loved ones left behind.
No vision of the morrow's strife
The warrior's dream alarms;
Nor braying horn, nor screaming fife
At dawn shall call to arms.

Their shivered swords are red with rust,
Their plumed heads are bowed,
Their haughty banner, trailed in dust,
Is now their martial shroud.
And plenteous funeral-tears have washed,
The red stains from each brow;
And the proud forms, by battle gashed,
Are freed from anguish now.

The neighing troop, the flashing blade,
The bugle's stirring blast,
The charge, the dreadful cannonade,
The din and shout are past.
Nor war's wild note, nor glory's peal,
Shall thrill with fierce delight
Those breasts that never more may feel
The rapture of the fight.

ALL QUIET ALONG THE POTOMAC

(The authorship of this poem has been disputed. It is ascribed to Lamar Fontaine, Second Virginia Cavalry.)

"All quiet along the Potomac tonight,"
Except now and then a stray picket
Is shot as he walks on his beat to and fro,
By a rifleman hid in the thicket.
'Tis nothing — a private or two now and then
Will not count in the news of the battle;
Not an officer lost — only one of the men —
Moaning out, all alone, the death rattle.

"All quiet along the Potomac tonight,"
Where the soldiers lie peacefully dreaming;
Their tents, in the rays of the clear autumn moon,
Or the light of the watch fires are gleaming,
A tremulous sigh, as the gentle night-wind
Through the forest leaves slowly is creeping,
While the stars up above, with their glittering eyes,
Keep guard — for the army is sleeping.

There is only the sound of the lone sentry's tread,
As he tramps from the rock to the fountain,
And thinks of the two in the low trundle bed,
Far away in the cot on the mountain.
His musket falls slack — his face, dark and grim,
Grows gentle with memories tender,
As he mutters a prayer for his children asleep —
For their mother, may heaven defend her!

The moon seems to shine as brightly as then,
That night, when the love yet unspoken
Leaped up to his lips, and when low murmured vows
Were pledged to be ever unbroken.
Then drawing his sleeve roughly over his eyes,
He dashes off tears that are welling,
And gathers his gun close up to its place,
As if to keep down the heart swelling.

He passes the fountain, the blasted pine tree —
The footstep is lagging and weary,
Yet onward he goes, through the broad belt of light,
Towards the shades of the forest so dreary.
Hark! was it the night-wind that rustled the leaves?
Was it moonlight so wondrously flashing?
It looked like a rifle — ha! Mary, goodbye!
And the life-blood is ebbing and splashing!

"All quiet along the Potomac tonight,"
No sound save the rush of the river;
While soft falls the dew on the face of the dead —
The picket's off duty forever.
1861

TO THE CONFEDERATE DEAD

Below we give the inscriptions upon the Confederate monument in the State Capitol Grounds, Columbia, S. C. erected by the women of South Carolina to the Confederate dead:

NORTH SIDE

This Monument
Perpetuates the Memory
of those Who,
True to the Instincts of their Birth,
Faithful to the Teachings of their Fathers,
Constant in their Love for the State,
Died in the Performance of their Duty;
Who have Glorified a Fallen Cause

Experience of a Confederate Chaplain 1861–1865

By the Simple Manhood of their Lives,
the Patient Endurance of Suffering,
and the Heroism of Death,
and who, in the Dark Hours of Imprisonment,
in the Hopelessness of the Hospital,
in the Short, Sharp Agony of the Field,
Found Support and Consolation in the Belief
that at home they would not be forgotten.

SOUTH SIDE

Let the Stranger
Who May in Future Times
Read this Inscription,
Recognize that these were Men
Whom Death Could not Terrify,
Whom Defeat Could not Dishonor,
and let their Virtues Plead.
for Just Judgment,
of the Cause in which they Perished.
Let the South Carolinian
of Another Generation
Remember
That the State Taught Them
How to Live and How to Die,
And that from her Broken Fortunes
She has Preserved for Her Children
the Priceless Treasure of their Memories,
Teaching all who may claim
the Same Birthright
that Truth, Courage, and Patriotism
Endure Forever.

LITTLE GIFFEN

Out of the focal and foremost fire,
Out of the hospital wall as dire,
Smitten of grape shot and gangrene,
(Eighteenth battle and he sixteen!)

Spectre! Such as you seldom see,
Little Giffen of Tennessee!

"Take him and welcome!" the surgeons said;
Little the doctor can help the dead!
So we took him and brought him where
The balm was sweet in the summer air;
And we laid him down on a wholesome bed —
Metter Lazarus, heel to head!

And we watched th« war with bated breath —
Skeleton boy against skeleton death.
Months of torture, how many such
Weary weeks of stick and crutch,
And still a glint of the steel-blue eye,
Told of a spirit that wouldn't die.

And didn't. Nay, more! in death's despite
The crippled skeleton "learned to write."
Dear Mother, at first, of course; and then
Dear Captain, inquiring about the men.
Captain's answer; of eighty and five,
Giffen and I are left alive.

Word of gloom from the war one day :
Johnston pressed at the front, they say.
Little Giffen was up and hurried away;
A tear — his first — as he bade goodbye,
Dimmed the glint of his steel-blue eye.
"I'll write, if spared!" There was news of the fight,
But none of Giffen — he did not write.

I sometimes fancy that, were I king
Of the princely knights of the Golden Ring,
With the song of the minstrel in mine ear,
And the tender story that trembles here,
I'd give the best on his bended knee,
The whitest soul of my chivalry,
For "Little Giffen" of Tennessee.

— *Frank O. Ticknor*

THE CONQUERED BANNER
Abram Joseph Ryan

Furl that banner, for 'tis weary,
'Round it's staff 'tis drooping dreary,
   Furl it, fold it, it is best;
For there's not a man to wave it,

And there's not a sword to save it;
And there's not one left to lave it,
In the blood which heroes gave it,
And it's foes now scorn and brave it;
   Furl it, hide it— let it rest!

Take that banner down! 'tis tattered?
Broken is its staff and shattered;
And the valiant hosts are scattered
   Over whom it floated high.
Oh! 'tis hard for us to fold it;
Hard to think there's none to hold it;
Hard that those who once unrolled it,
   Now must furl it with a sigh.

Furl that banner! Furl it sadly!
Once ten thousand hailed it gladly,
And ten thousand wildly, madly;
   Swore it should forever wave;
Swore that foeman's sword should never
Hearts like theirs entwined dissever,
Till that flag should float forever
   O'er their freedom or their grave!

Furl it I For the hands that grasped it;
And the hearts that fondly clasped it,
   Cold and dead are lying low;
And that banner — it is trailing!
While around it sounds the wailing
   Of its people in their woe.
For though conquered, they adore it?

Love the cold, dead hands that bore it!
Weep for those who fell before it!
Pardon those who trailed and tore it!
But, oh! wildly they deplore it!
No w who furl and fold it so.

Furl that banner! True, 'tis gory,
Yet 'tis wreathed around with glory;
And 'twill live in song and story,
　　Though it's folds are in the dust;
For it's fame on brightest pages,
Penned by poets and by sages,
Shall go sounding down the ages —
　　Furl it's folds though now we must.

Furl that banner, softly, slowly,
Treat it gently — it is holy —
　　For it droops above the dead,
Touch it not — unfold it never,
Let it droop there, furled forever,
　　For its people's hopes are dead!

DIXIE

Air: "Annie Laurie"

Oh! Dixie's homes are bonnie,
　　And Dixie's hearts are true;
And 'twas down in dear old Dixie
　　Our life's first breath we drew;
(And there our last we sigh),
　　And for Dixie, dear old Dixie,

We'll lay us down and die.
　　No fairer land than Dixie's
Has ever seen the light;
　　No braver boys than Dixie's
To stand for Dixie's right;
　　(With hearts so true and high),
And for Dixie, dear old Dixie,
　　To lay them down and die.

Experience of a Confederate Chaplain 1861–1865

Oh! Dixie's vales are sunny,
    And Dixie's hills are blue,
And Dixie's skies are bonnie,
    And Dixie's daughters, too —
(As stars in Dixie's sky)
    And for Dixie, dear old Dixie,
We'll lay us down and die.

No more upon the mountain,
    No longer by the shore,
The trumpet song of Dixie
    Shall shake the world no more;
For Dixie's songs are o'er,
    Her glory gone on high,
And the brave who bled for Dixie,
    Have laid them down to die.

          — F. O. Ticknor of Columbus, Ga.

LAND OF THE SOUTH

Land of the South! — Imperial land!
    How proud thy mountains rise! —
How sweet thy scenes on every hand!
    How fair thy covering skies!
But not for this — oh, not for these,
    I love thy fields to roam —
Thou hast a dearer spell to me —
    Thou art my native home!

The rivers roll their liquid wealth,
    Unequaled to the sea —
Thy hills and valleys bloom with health,
    And green with verdure be!
But, not for thy proud ocean streams,
    Not for thine azure dome —
Sweet, sunny South! — I cling to thee —
    Thou art my native home!

I've stood beneath Italia's clime
    Beloved of tale and song —
On Helvyn's hills, proud and sublime,
    Where nature's wonders throng;
By Tempe's classic sunlit streams,
    Where gods of old did roam —
But ne'er have found so fair a land
    As thee — my native home!

And thou hast prouder glories, too,
    Than nature ever gave, —
Peace sheds o'er thee her genial dew
    And Freedom's pinions wave,
Fair science flings her pearls around —
    Religion lifts her dome —
These, these endear thee to my heart, —
    My own, loved native home!

And "heaven's best gift to man" is thine, —
    God bless thy rosy girls!
Like sylvan flowers, they shine,
    Their hearts are pure as pearls!
And grace and goodness circle them,
    Where'er their footsteps roam. —
How can I then, whilst loving them,
    Not love my native home?

Land of the South! Imperial land! —
    Then here's a health to thee, —
Long as thy mountain barriers stand,
    May'st thou be blest and free!
May dark dissension's banner ne'er
    Wave e'er thy fertile loam, —
But should it come, there's one will die
    To save his native home!

— Alexander Beaufort Meek,
Columbia, S. C.

THE OLD NORTH STATE
By Judge William Gaston

Carolina! Carolina! Heaven's blessings attend her!
    While we live we will cherish and love and defend her.
Though the scorner may sneer at and witlings defame her.
    Our hearts swell with gladness, whenever we name her.

    CHORUS: Hurrah! hurrah! The Old North State forever!
        Hurrah! hurrah! The good old North State!

Though she envies not others their merited glory,
    Say, whose name stands the foremost in Liberty's story?
Though too true to herself e'er to crouch to oppression,
    Who can yield to just rule a more loyal submission:'

Plain and artless her sons, but whose doors open faster
    At the knock of the stranger, or the tale of disaster?
How like to the rudeness of their dear native mountains —
    With rich ore in their bosoms and life in their fountains!

And her daughters, the queen of the forest resembling,
    So graceful, so constant, yet to gentlest breath trembling:
And, true lightwood at heart, let the match be applied them;
    How they kindle and flame! Oh! none know but who've tried them!

Then let all who love us, love the land that we live in —
    As happy a region as on this side of heaven —
Where plenty and freedom, love and peace smile before us,
    Raise aloud, raise together, the heart-thrilling chorus:

    Hurrah! hurrah! The old North State forever!
    Hurrah! hurrah! The good old North State!

HO! FOR CAROLINA!

Let no heart in sorrow weep for other days;
Let no idle dreamers tell in melting lays
Of the merry meetings in the rosy bowers —
For there's no land on earth like this fair land of ours!

CHORUS: Ho! for Carolina! that's the land for me!
In her happy borders roam the brave and free,
And her bright-eyed daughters! none can fairer be —
Oh! it is the land of love and sweet liberty!

Down in Carolina grows the lofty pine,
And her groves and forests bear the scented vine;
Here are peaceful homes, too, nestling 'mid the flowers—
Oh! there's no land on earth like this fair land of ours.

Come to Carolina in the summer time,
When the luscious fruits are hanging in their prime,
And the maidens singing in the leafy bowers —
Oh! there's no land on earth like this fair land of ours!

Her patriot sons are peaceful, modest, too, and brave,
The first to spurn the shackles intended for the slave;
Disdaining boastful tyrants, they trust in duty's powers —
Oh! there are no men on earth more nobly true than ours!

All her girls are charming, graceful, too, and gay,
Happy as the blue-birds in the month of May;
And they steal your hearts by their magic powers—
Oh! there are no girls on earth that can compare with ours!

Behold her vales and forests, her sparkling brooks and rills,
And fields of golden harvests, her mountains and her hills,
All robed in fairest beauty with nature's sweetest flowers —
Oh! who would not be proud of this heritage of ours?

— *Anonymous*

"APPLES OF GOLD IN PICTURES OF SILVER"
Affectionately Dedicated to Papa
By W. A. B.

A stranger passing on the streets of Frederick, Maryland,
Was marching with a Southern corps, a brave and war-like band.
By chance he saw a sight full pure enough for heaven's dome,
Which made his heart leap forth with joy in tender thought of home.

A little maiden pure and sweet seemed flitting through the air,
Transformed into an angel bright, with brow untouched by care.
Her hand of mercy seized a cup filled with sparkling water,
And poured well full the soldier's tins, like a queenly daughter.

A vessel near was kept supplied with the refreshing draught,
And as she worked with hands of love, so merrily she laughed.
A chaplain of the "Thirtieth" (this stranger passing by)
Stood rapt, in meditation on the sight which met his eye.

He gazed with fond devotion as his trembling hand he laid
Upon her youthful head and said, "God bless you, little maid!"
"He will bless you, for he hath said whoever shall e'en give
A cup of water in his name, shall a reward receive."

He went his way, absorbed in thought, when suddenly in rear
He heard a little pit-a-pat upon the sidewalk near.
Facing about he met the maid, who sweetly said: "Mister,
Mama says will you please come back there, just a moment, sir?"

She led him through this door and that, through passage, hall and out
Into a parlor, large and bright-garbed in his "round-about."
A lady rose with queenly grace, who said: "Kind sir," you spoke
Unto my little girl just now, God's blessings to invoke."

The stranger bowed with modest air in assent to the same,
And then with guests and relatives a moment's chat they claim.
The chaplain leaves. He bids adieu to friends collected there
And joins his comrades on the march, the crown to win and wear.

* * * * * * * * *

The war is o'er. In "Sixty-six," on N. C.'s eastern shore,
Is found an humble Pastor who is weary and foot-sore.
The ills of war have plied too well their scourge with iron hand
And Carolina's goodly soil is desolated land.

The Pastor, too, partakes of this misfortune of his State.
Chill penury applies with pain her comfort-less ill-fate.
His little ones about him are in almost threadbare clothes;
And other bare necessities the pantry also shows.

We find him on a summer eve engaged in garden work,
Intent that he will persevere, nor e'en one duty shirk.
When lo, a lad calls at the gate! "A letter, sir!" he said.
The Pastor took the missive brought, then broke the seal and read.

He learned it was from distant friends of Frederick, Maryland,
And brought glad tidings to his heart, as sent by Mercy's hand.
His nerves gave way; o'ercome with joy at such outlook for fate,
He sought a stump which stood near by — his thoughts to collocate.

He reads that friends, in thoughtful love, their very best have done,
And that a box of "sundries" have been shipped to Wilmington.
That night around the household hearth, to Our Father's care
These "friends indeed" were wafted up in humble, heart-felt prayer.

Bost's Mills, Cabarrus County, N. C., July 14th, 1876

Experience of a Confederate Chaplain 1861–1865

Rev. W. A. Betts, Ph. B. (University of N. C.)

Methodist Episcopal Church, South
South Carolina Conference

Experience of a Confederate Chaplain 1861–1865

Lincoln As The South Should Know Him
....O. W. Blacknall

Truth of the War Conspiracy of 1861
....H. W. Johnstone

A Story Behind Every Stone
.... Charles E. Purser

As You May Never See Us Again
.... Joel Craig and Sharlene Baker

Additional Information and Amendments to the North Carolina Troops 1861 – 1865 Volume I & II
.... Charles E. Purser

Memoir of Nathaniel Macon of North Carolina......... Weldon N. Edwards

Sherman's Rascals..Frank B. Powell, III

A Southern View of the Invasion of the Southern States and War of 1861-65 .... Captain Samuel A. Ashe

A Confederate Catechism ....Lyon Gardiner Tyler

General Robert E. Lee.. Captain Samuel A. Ashe

General Lee and Santa Claus...Louise Clack

The Life of Nathaniel Macon ....William E. Dodd

The Land We Love — The South and It's Heritage........... Dr. Boyd Cathey

Experience of a Confederate Chaplain 1861–1865

Pickett or Pettigrew? An Historical Essay.....................Captain W. R. Bond

A View of the Constitution of the United States of America
....William Rawle

The Confederate Myth-Buster.. Walter D. Kennedy

Confederate States Military Prison at Salisbury, NC... Dr. A. W. Mangum

Red State — Red County..James R. Kennedy

Some Things For Which The South Did Not Fight
.... Dr. Henry Tucker Graham

The Retribution Conspiracy... Samuel W. Mitcham

Little Sermons in Socialism by Abraham Lincoln ....Burke McCarty

Roster of North Carolinians in Confederate Naval Service
.... LTC. (Retired) Sion H. Harrington, III

Words of Love ....Rev. Dr. W. Herman White

The Constitution of the Confederate States of America

The Adventure — Stolen Days ....Mark Vogl

The Life of General Robert E. Lee In Easy Words For Children
.... Mrs. Mary L. Williamson

Sketch of the Twelfth Alabama Infantry.........Captain Robert Emory Park

More information available at
www.scuppernongpress.com

The Scuppernong Press
PO Box 1724
Wake Forest, NC 27588

www.ingramcontent.com/pod-product-compliance
Lightning Source LLC
Chambersburg PA
CBHW050513240426
43673CB00004B/204